First Edition

Cover design by M.A.Shine
Interior Art by Kerian Massey - keriansart.com

Special thanks to R, for tolerating this work's completion

This book was printed on 100% recycled pixels

How To Pass Your INFOSEC Certification Test

If you're a professional in the field of IT, IT security, audit, or general security, you know that certifications are the key to better job opportunities and higher pay. There are many available, from various sources; many of them come from manufacturers and vendors of specific products, many from certification bodies and organizations, and some from government and quasi-government sources. The certifications usually require that you pass a multiple-choice test.

This book is meant to help you pass these tests. It contains lists and descriptions of material usually tested, regardless of certifier or test.

I have the CISSP, CCSP, CISM, and Security+ certifications, and used to hold the SANS GSEC. I've taught prep courses for most of them, and am familiar with material that shows up over and over again, on all of them. I'm not an expert in any single area of IT or INFOSEC, nor am I even all that smart....but I am good at passing multiple-choice tests, and I am told that I'm good at conveying information. So I'm offering that knowledge to you.

I hope you find this book useful. If, after you take the test, you are unable to pass, and you think this book did not help you prepare for it, get in touch with me, and I'll refund you half the cost of the book. I want you to feel like you received value for your money. I'll even include a list of all those people who have asked for refunds, in each subsequent edition of this book.

This book is not a standalone product: you won't be able to read the book and just pass the test. The book is designed for practitioners in the field: people who have trained and worked in INFOSEC for some time, who have the background and essentials to get the certifications. In addition to the book, you should be reviewing other sources (especially the sourcebook from the certifying body for the test you're taking), including sample tests, primary sources, other books, classes, and online content. This book will show you the information you need to know, but you may have to do some additional research to get more comprehensive details about that information; I recommend Wikipedia and other online sources, because they are both exhaustive and -often- free.

I hope the book helps you pass your exam and get your certification. Please let me know what you think of it, whether you think it helped your study efforts or if you know some way it could be improved. Good luck!

Chapter 1: The Basics
Chapter 2: Encryption
Chapter 3: Regulation, Legal, and Privacy
Chapter 4: Personnel and Training
Chapter 5: Tech
Chapter 6: Academics
Chapter 7: Physical
Chapter 8: Incidents and Disasters
Chapter 9: Taking Tests

Chapter 1: The Basics

There are certain INFOSEC fundamentals you should know thoroughly.

Terms:

BYOD: "bring your own device"; an enterprise environment where users are allowed to use personally-owned devices to access the organization's data and resources.

defense-in-depth: Also known as "layered defense," the practice of using multiple kinds of controls of differing types to protect something.

DLP: Data loss prevention or data leak protection, or any combination of those terms. A tool used to monitor/prevent data leaving the control of the organization; egress monitoring.

DOS/denial of service: loss of availability; can be imposed from external factors or caused internally, inadvertently or maliciously

DDOS/distributed denial of service: loss of availability due to a "botnet"; a group of machines that have been compromised by an attacker for the purpose of causing an outage

HTTP: Hypertext Transfer Protocol. The set of formats and instructions for Web-based communication.

ISO: The International Standards Organization. A body that publishes standards. While recognized worldwide, the ISO standards are particularly important in Europe, where local laws often require that businesses comply with specific ISO standards. ISO standards are often comprehensive, thorough, and quite expensive to implement and certify.

> **Truly Deep**
> When creating a strategy of defense-in-depth, it's not enough to have multiple controls for protection; it's important to use a variety of kinds of controls as well. Your security plan should include physical, administrative, and logical controls, of differing technological levels, in order to thoroughly protect your assets.

layered defense: see "defense-in-depth"

malware: literally, malicious software; viruses, worms, Trojan horse applications, etc.

NIST: The United States National Institute of Standards and Technology. Under the Department of Commerce, NIST publishes many IT-centric standards and guides (usually called either Special Publications (SPs) or Federal Information Processing Standards (FIPS)). NIST publications are usually informative, well-written, and unlike some other standards accepted in the IT field (particularly the ISO standards), completely free of charge. While NIST publications are specifically written for federal government entities, they can be easily adapted for use in the private sector, and are still recognized as acceptable for the purpose.

nonrepudiation: the sender of a message cannot deny sending that message; a property offered by asymmetric encryption and digital signatures

residual risk: the risk that remains after risk mitigation efforts have been enacted

risk: the possibility of harm; the likelihood that a threat will exploit a vulnerability

risk acceptance: opting to continue operations with the inherent level of risk; this can be done in conjunction with and after risk mitigation efforts

risk appetite: the level of risk an organization is willing to accept in order to operate; this is decided by senior management, and is different for every organization

Name Game
Our industry is horrible with naming conventions/taxonomy. We name things with the same words and abbreviations [How many meanings can you think of in the IT field for the homonyms "MAC"/"Mac"?] You'll have to use context clues for some of the questions, in order to determine which meaning the test is asking for.

risk avoidance: opting to refrain from an activity because the risk exceeds the organization's risk appetite

risk mitigation: attempts to reduce risk, usually through the use of controls

risk transfer: paying some other entity to take liability for risky operations; basically, this means buying insurance

threat: something that poses the possibility of harm; this could be a malicious attacker, a natural event, an emergency situation, etc.

vulnerability: a possible avenue of loss or harm; this can be a gap in your security, or it can be a facet of your enterprise, or it can be a fault in the design of a product or service

The Triad

The CIA Triad is fundamental to INFOSEC. You can be sure that more than one question on your test will deal with the Triad and its components.

Confidentiality: data is protected from being viewed unintentionally.

Integrity: data is not changed accidentally or maliciously.

Availability: the data can be accessed (within limits of permitted use and authorization/authentication).

In most instances, questions will deal with aspects of the Triad...you may be asked what parts of the Triad are supported by encryption (Confidentiality and Integrity, not Availability), for example. Be able to think through the various threats, vulnerabilities, risks, and attacks and know which part of the Triad they can/would affect.

> **Trick Question**
> Tests often include a question about which parts of the Triad are protected by cryptographic hashes; this is often a trick question, because the answer is Confidentiality and Integrity, but not Availability...hashes can also offer nonrepudiation and authentication, which are not normally considered part of the Triad, but are often addressed in exams.

Don't overthink questions that pertain to the Triad; it's very easy to stretch concepts past the point where they make sense, but most exams control for that sort of thing. For instance, I've seen written work that justifies encryption as a means to protect Availability, because (the tortured logic goes) if an attacker steals your data or deletes it, the data will no longer be Available. That's a twice-removed causation at best, and not a correct application of the concept. But, again: most tests are not ridiculous, and the majority of questions are very fair, so you shouldn't try to think past the most reasonable response to Triad questions.

In many cases, the proper response to a Triad question will be another leg of the Triad, because the question asks about one or two of them. Whenever you see any of the three, be ready to answer with another or both of the other two.

Concepts:

Least privilege: We only give people the minimal amount of permissions/access necessary to do their jobs. For instance, we don't give sysadmins administrative control of network devices; that is only granted to network admins...who usually aren't given system administration permissions on user devices. In fact, sysadmins might not even get physical access to network devices. This limits the exposure, and therefore the risk. And we don't give users ***anything***. Maybe a banana.

Separation of duties: For any given business process, two or more people should be involved. The classic example is purchasing/acquisition: nothing can be bought for the organization unless at least two people - say, the manager of the department making the purchase, and the accounting department rep who cuts the check- add their signatures to the purchase order and the check. This helps cut down on corruption.

Dual control: In the military, this is referred to as Two-Person Integrity, and sometimes Dual Key (not to be confused with cryptography keys-- I'll cover that later). Two people are necessary to gain access/control of data. For example, data might be stored in a safe with two different locks, each with different combinations, and each combination is given to only half the people in the office. That way, one member of each group needs to take part in opening the safe and getting the data. Again, this should deter unauthorized access. It's similar to the notion of separation duties in that it involves two people, but it's a very different concept. Think of it this way: separation of duties is about deterring corruption during a *process*, and dual control is about deterring unauthorized *access*.

Job rotation: It's good policy to have personnel perform duties and tasks assigned to various roles in the office over the course of a year. This mitigates malicious action, because dishonest activity might be detected when a fresh set of eyes takes over a certain task, and also provides redundancy of capabilities among your personnel.

Mandatory leave: Very similar to job rotation-- if someone is doing something nefarious, and it has not been detected, sending them away from the office and letting someone else perform that task allows an opportunity to uncover wrongdoing. Also, it's much better for morale.

Do not oversecure: I am not sure how to emphasize this idea strongly enough. **DO NOT OVERSECURE.** There is a tendency to put controls on everything, to deny all exceptions to policy, to prohibit any changes...and this deters operations. Security supports the business needs of the organization...and security is always a tradeoff with operations: the more secure something is, the more expensive and less efficient it becomes. So resist the urge for enacting excess controls, and let the business needs and risk appetite of

the organization be your guide. You should not put a
$10 lock on a $5 bicycle.

Policy:

Everything flows from policy. A mature
environment will have policies for just about every
facet of security-- the overall security program policy,
a personnel security policy, policies for data
management/handling/retention/destruction/labeling,
physical security policy, access policy, acceptable use
policy, security controls policy, and so on. The exam
will ask certain things about policy
promulgation/dissemination/drafting. Here are some of
the things you can expect:

Policy generation and acceptance: Policies have
to start at some point; every policy is new to begin
with. When creating policy, certain activities will
increase the likelihood that new policies are accepted
by the organization as a whole and users in general.
These include:

- Senior management buy-in. When the
leaders of the organization support and
follow the policy, it's much more likely
for all users to take the policy seriously.

- Inclusion of all stakeholders in crafting
the policy. Every office should be
represented in the formative stages of
creating policies, and so should every
group within the organization (including
users, who need a voice in the process).

- Explanation and informed user base. If people know the reasons for the rules, they're more likely to follow them. See Chapter 4: Personnel and Training.

- Simplicity of language and ease of use. This is tied to understanding; if policies include a lot of jargon (especially legalese or technobabble), most people in the organization won't be able to understand them.

- POLICIES MUST BE TIED TO OPERATIONAL GOALS. This is a recurring theme in security, and on the exams. If your security policies get in the way of people trying to do their jobs, they will violate your policies and make your environment less secure by finding ways around the restrictions.

Policy legitimacy: Policies can't conflict with existing legislation or legal precedents, and should not conflict with known, accepted standards. You also need to ensure that all your personnel acknowledge receipt and understanding of the policies, and that the policies include a thorough explanation of enforcement methodology and potential consequences for violating policies.

> **Play on Words:**
> "Policy" and "governance" are not exactly the same thing, but go ahead and treat the terms as synonyms for purposes of the test.

Documentation: Record everything. Keep a set of notes about the policies, explaining why the organization chose to make the policy decisions it did, and --just as importantly-- keep a record of why the organization to *against* certain choices. This will be helpful when you revisit and review your policies.

Exceptions: A policy is not a religious doctrine; each policy should not be so inflexible as to never allow for variations. When drafting policy, include phrasing about how to approve exceptions, and how and where all exceptions will be listed.

Review and evolution: Policies should not be set in stone, especially in our industry, which changes quickly and extensively. Policies must be kept current with events in our field, new regulation, and technological developments. Check your policies at LEAST annually. Update as needed. Keep a revision history.

Types of Controls:

Detective: Just like it sounds. A detective control notices a threat being realized, and may communicate the activity (usually to security personnel). A detective control might be an intrusion alarm system or a smoke detector or an IDS.

Preventive: Again, the word describes the control well. Prevents the threat from exploiting a vulnerability. Examples of preventive controls might be concrete exterior walls, shutting down specific ports and services, or bollards. Also referred to as "preventative"-- the terms are synonymous.

Deterrent: Works somewhat like preventive controls; discourages attacks simply by existing. Concertina wire might be a deterrent control, as could a posted notice or user agreement regarding monitoring and punitive action.

Corrective: A control that takes action upon detecting an ongoing attack or failed security state. An IPS might be considered corrective, in that it takes programmed action in response to detecting malicious traffic by automatically shutting down a port or service or halting a connection (as opposed to an IDS, which only sends the alert).

> **Fuzziness.**
> **There are no hard-and-fast dictates which group controls into specific types, and arguments could be made for some controls belonging to several families. For instance, is a surveillance camera detective or preventive? Or is it possibly a deterrent? If it's hooked up to your SEIM/SIM/SEM, is it physical or logical?**
>
> **The answer, sadly, is, "yes."**

Compensating: A control that makes up for the failure of another control. Often used in good planning of a layered defense strategy. Also sometimes called "compensatory."

Physical: Those controls that act in the tangible world. Doors, locks, fences, guards.

Administrative: Policy controls. An access control motif based around roles or rules can be considered an administrative control, as could an Acceptable Use Policy (AUP) or a background check.

Technical: Sometimes called "logical controls"; electronic and IT-based controls. Antimalware software, IDS/IPSs, firewalls, etc.

Chapter 2: Encryption

Encryption accounts for a high percentage of questions on INFOSEC exams because questions about encryption are really easy to write; there are objective, discrete answers to many encryption questions, which is different from many of the other testable topics. On top of that, encryption is used for so many purposes in our field, for both data at rest and data in motion, and is somehow seen as a magic bullet by senior management: they don't really understand encryption, but have heard about it, so often request or suggest implementation for any and all purposes. So you are likely to see a significant number of encryption-related questions on any INFOSEC-related certification exam. This chapter will list possible encryption topics you might see, without going into too much detail. Be prepared to study a bit more about each topic to cover it thoroughly enough to pass the exam.

Encryption Basics

Cryptography is about taking a message and modifying it in some way so that only the intended recipient can understand it. There are many ways to do this, but modern crypto is about running the message through a cryptosystem, which results in a message that can only be decrypted by someone else who has the same system. Math is involved.

Know the following terms--

Plaintext: The message before it is encrypted. Our example will be: "The exam is easy."

Ciphertext: The message after encryption. Ciphertext of the example might be: "FUEIIEDLKNDWLS." But not really, because it's just gibberish I got from mashing the keyboard, not anything that comes from a cryptosystem.

Encryption: The act of garbling plaintext to ciphertext.

Decryption: Converting ciphertext back to plaintext.

Encryption keys: The secret element of a cryptosystem, the part that is not shared with anyone other than the parties to the communication. The work factor of a cryptosystem can be enhanced by increasing the key strength; that is, by increasing the length of the keys, or repeating them less frequently in the encryption/decryption process, or introducing variables. Modern cryptosystems favor extremely long key lengths to assure a longer work factor.

> **Piece of Nerd History**
> The popular "Ultima" computer game series used simple substitution as a rudimentary form of digital rights management, replacing important game information with gibberish from a made-up alphabet.

Simple substitution: An archaic form of crypto where the characters are replaced with another set (or sets) of characters. A famous substitution cipher was the Caesar Cipher, or ROT 13, which involved rotating each character 13 spaces through the alphabet. So our example in ciphertext, via ROT 13, would be: "Gur rknz vf rnfl." Substitution can be done with invented alphabets, too. Substitution is very vulnerable to cracking, because of the logical occurrence of each letter in a language.

Transposition: Shifting the position of characters in a message to garble it. The Greek scytale is a historical example often mentioned in exam prep, as is the rail fence method. The example, after suffering a transposition, might look like: "Texmsayheaies." Also vulnerable to modern cracking efforts.

One-time pads: A form of encryption where each party involved has a shared secret that is used -get this- only once. If used properly, one-time pads cannot be cracked.

Work factor: The measure of the strength of a cryptosystem, in units of time. Literally, the amount of time it would take a non-nation-state actor to crack a given cryptosystem using brute force.

Block size: One way to encrypt information is the parse out the full message in smaller, easy-to-handle chunks of characters; these are called "blocks." Like with the encryption keys, the longer (in number of characters) a block, the higher the work factor for that cryptosystem.

Symmetric vs. Asymmetric

Think of the root word: symmetry.

Symmetric encryption uses the same key for encryption and decryption

Asymmetric encryption uses two or more different keys for encryption and decryption.

Symmetric encryption is also known as "shared secret" cryptography. Both parties have the same key, but nobody else besides the two of them know it. The difficult aspect of symmetric encryption is getting the key securely from one party to another. Usually, the key is passed by a mechanism other than the method by which they plan to communicate; this is called passing the key "out of band." So if the parties are going to communicate, for instance, via telecommunications, they might choose to deliver the key in written form, by hand, via a secure courier. This can get expensive and cumbersome, and requires an existing, secure method of communication to create a new secure method of communication.

In public-key encryption, the parties involved in secure communication each have a pair of keys: one public key, which can be shared with anyone; and one private key, which is retained and held confidential by each party. They exchange their public keys with each other, then can engage in secure communication by encrypting messages with either or both the public keys. Each party can use their own private key to decrypt messages encrypted with their corresponding public key.

The classic explanation has Alice and Bob trading public keys to send secure messages. Alice gives her public key to Bob, and Bob gives his public key to Alice. When Alice wants to send a secure message to Bob, she encrypts it with Bob's public key and sends the encrypted message to Bob. Bob can decrypt it with his private key. There are also all sorts of fancy permutations, where they can do things like sign messages with their private keys in order to prove authenticity and so forth.

> Alice and Bob have been sending each other secure messages for over 30 years. I am convinced they are having an affair.

Diffie-Hellman Key Exchange: This a technique whereby two parties can use asymmetric encryption to create a shared secret for symmetric encryption. Diffie-Hellman key exchange is often used to create temporary session keys for specific conversations, which are then never used again.

Hashes: A hash is a one-way encryption: a message is run through a hashing algorithm, which creates a shorter, undecryptable digest of the original. When the hash is sent to a recipient along with plaintext of the message, the recipient can run the plaintext through the same algorithm and see if the two hashes are exactly the same; any slight modification to the original message will result in a different hash. Hashes, therefore, provide a means to verify the integrity of a message, but not confidentiality or availability.

> **Good Hash**
> We call the hashing algorithm a "hash function," and when we run the message through a hash function, we call the result a "message digest," a "digest," or sometimes just a "hash."

Digital Signatures: Asymmetric encryption can be used to support authentication, integrity, and nonrepudiation in communications. A sender can use their private key to "sign" a message hash by encrypting it and sending it along with the original plaintext, and the recipient can verify the sender and the integrity of the message by using the sender's public key. Again, this does not promote confidentiality of the message (the plaintext usually travels along with the signed hash).

PKI

Public-Key Infrastructure (PKI) is a mechanism for having third-party authentication/certificate-issue/digital signatures. The process can seem daunting and tricky to understand, so here's what you need to know for the test:

Certificate Authority (CA): Issues certificates, binding identities to certificate holders by using the holders' public keys (from a public-private key pair, where the certificate holder keeps the private key private); the certificates are also signed with the private key of the CA. The CA can a privately-held structure within an organization, with certificates passed among that organization's personnel and assets, or a trusted third party entity allowing people and organizations that have never met and have no other direct relationship to establish a level of trust.

Registration Authority (RA): An entity that authenticates entities making requests for certificates. Some CAs are their own RAs; some CAs take authentication from independent RAs.

> **Fact: Many of the encryption "failures" that led to data breaches were due not to a cracked or outdated encryption mechanisms, but because of incorrect implementations of those cryptosystems.**

Certificate Revocation List (CRL): Just like it sounds-- a list of certificates that have been revoked. Certificates can be revoked for a number of reasons, such as a specific person leaving the employ of a company, or the accidental disclosure of a private key by a certificate holder. In all cases, certificates should have a finite lifespan (usually around two years), so that anyone who has a certificate is required to re-authenticate after a while, and just hold the same certificate in perpetuity.

Digital certificates: A set of characteristics describing the entity holding the certificate, in a format dictated by the X.509 standard.

Encryption Standards

The exams often contain questions about encryption standards and algorithms, past and present. Unfortunately, these questions are favorites of exam writers because the answers to questions about specific cryptosystems are discrete and concise (example: "What is the key length of the original DES cipher?"; answer: "Who cares? We use Triple DES now, because DES is old and the key length obviously wasn't long enough").

This is sad for you, because you're going to have to memorize the key lengths associated with specific standards and algorithms, including some we don't use anymore. I'm sorry. But it's not my fault.

Memorize these:

Data Encryption Standard (DES): 56-bit key with 8 parity bits, and 64-bit blocks

Triple DES (3DES): 168-, 112-, or 56-bit keys, and 64-bit blocks

Blowfish: key sizes ranging from 32 to 448 bits, 64-bit blocks

Twofish: keys of 128, 192, or 256 bits, and 128-bit blocks

Advanced Encryption Standard (AES): Originally called Rijndael. Block size 128; key lengths of 128, 192, and 256.

Secure Hashing Algorithm (SHA):

SHA-1: 160-bit hash; no longer approved

SHA-2: hash outputs ranging from 224 bits to 512 bits, depending on implementation

SHA-3: same hash lengths as SHA-2

Message Digest 5 (MD5): 128-bit outputs; subject to many vulnerabilities

RSA: asymmetric cryptosystem based on factoring two large prime numbers, with key sizes ranging from 1024 bits to 4096

NIST publishes a list of algorithms and standards which are currently acceptable, as well as those which have been outmoded:
http://csrc.nist.gov/groups/STM/cavp/validation.html

Chapter 3: Regulation, Legal, and Privacy

A lot of what we do is based on statutes, standards, precedence, and other forms of regulation. Our policies and governance should take these into account, and mimic them in many ways. Unfortunately, in our field, developments outpace the legislative process to a ridiculous degree; the law is always catching up to the tech (and the use of the tech). So we're often stuck using archaic and outmoded laws. Such is the nature of our biz.

These are some of the laws/regulations/standards you can expect to see on the exam:

- The EU Data Directive (and yes, Safe Harbor): EU Directive 95/46/EC addresses the rights of EU citizens regarding their personal information (PII, in general). The Data Directive was superseded in May 2016, but it still remains a topic on many exams, so you need to know it. Specific points you need to know about the EU Directive:

-- No company outside the EU is allowed to store/process/collect PII from EU citizens.

Exceptions:

--- If the country where the company resides has a law that matches all conditions of the EU Data Directive. For instance, Argentina has such a law, and is recognized by the EU accordingly.

--- If the country where the company resides has a Safe Harbor program. The Safe Harbor program allows developed countries to create a voluntary list of companies that agree to subscribe to the EU Directive, and agree to oversight by a government entity that serves as the Safe Harbor enforcer in that country. For instance, in the US (which does not have a law that matches the EU Directive), the Safe Harbor program is administered by the Department of Commerce (except for companies in certain industries, such as airlines and shipping firms, which fall under the Department of Transportation).

--- If the company creates its own policy that upholds all elements of the EU Directive. If the company is a multinational, it must file for permission to operate in accordance with the EU Directive in *each* EU country where the company has an office.

> **Exit Strategy**
> All the exam questions were written before Brexit, so none of that will be on the test.

-- For EU citizens, privacy is not just a notion, it is a human right. This right includes the Right To Be Forgotten; any EU citizen can contact any entity that has any of their PII data and demand it all be deleted, permanently. This has been challenged and upheld by the highest court in the EU. [As far as I know, the Right To Be Forgotten does not include data held by law enforcement agencies.]

National Security
Some countries wrote and ratified privacy laws specifically to conform to the EU Data Directive, and some had existing privacy laws that fulfill the Data Directive requirements. These are worth knowing for the exam: **Argentina, Australia/New Zealand, Israel, Canada, Switzerland, Singapore, and Japan.**

- The American federal data privacy law: There is no overall data privacy law in the US. There are some industry-specific and sector-specific laws (mentioned below), but no federal statute that addresses PII in the private sector.

-- HIPAA: The Health Information Portability and Accountability Act allows Americans to review, correct, and restrict dissemination of their Electronic Protected Health Information (ePHI: basically, PII from a medical perspective). HIPAA addresses medical providers that regularly conduct electronic transactions of medical data, and associated businesses that might get ePHI from medical providers.

-- GLBA: The Graham-Leach-Bliley Act covers privacy information of financial service customers. This includes PII and account information for customers of banks, insurance companies, credit services, and similar entities. GLBA requires that financial service providers protect customer data, and also requires that these companies get written customer consent before sharing any of that data.

-- FERPA: The Family Educational Rights and Privacy Act recognizes the rights of parents (and adult students) to control, review, and correct their student information. This does not give the right to collect damages from breach, but does allow students and parents to hold schools accountable to regulators.

-- SOX: The Sarbanes-Oxley Act addresses financial reporting for publically-traded companies and the firms that service them (such as accountants, auditors, and consultants). The portions of SOX that affect our field come from requirements to implement operational controls and protect data.

-- PCI-DSS: The Payment Card Industry Data Security Standard is a contractual regulation, not a law; it was created and is promulgated by the major credit card companies. Any merchant that accepts credit card payments is necessarily obligated to comply with this standard. PCI DSS mandates that merchants protect cardholder data, to include encrypting it and destroying it at the end of its use. The standard specifies a three-tiered structure of participants, based on number and value of annual transactions, and is comprehensive and descriptive in describing control mechanisms.

-- COPPA/CIPA: Two federal laws that are intended to protect children on the Internet. The Children's Online Privacy Protection Act (COPPA) limits how websites can market to and collect data from children under the age of 13. The Children's Internet Protection Act (CIPA) mandates that all schools and libraries must use Web filtering tools to limit children's access to adult material online.

- Oh, Canada. Canada has a privacy law called PIPEDA, which is almost exactly the EU Data Directive, verbatim. They probably pronounce any word with "ou" as "oo," though, when reading it aloud.

- APEC. The Asian-Pacific Economic Cooperation council (APEC) is a pro-trade organization made up of 21 member countries in the Pacific Rim. This is a non-treaty entity, so none of their doctrine is legally binding, but it may appear on exams. What you need to know is: APEC is a strong supporter of free trade, and endorses strong privacy controls as a means to encourage individuals to participate in commerce (the rationale is: if people trust businesses and governments to protect everyone's private information, then people will engage in more commercial activity, which makes sense).

- Argentina. As was mentioned twice already, Argentina is noteworthy for having a national privacy law that adheres to the EU Data Directive. Remember that.
SSAE 16

From the American Institute of CPAs (AICPA), the SSAE 16 is the standard and reporting methodology for service organizations (read: auditing/accounting/consulting firms) to follow when preparing or reviewing financial reporting documents for most of their customers (read: publicly-traded companies that have to file such reports with the SEC, such as the 10-K and whatnot). This standard came about as a result of Sarbanes-Oxley (SOX), which was itself a response to a lot of skullduggery performed by publically-traded corporations in their own financial reports.

Here's what you need to know about the three kinds of SSAE 16 reports:

- SOC 1: These audits examine the company's financial reporting controls. From an IT security perspective, this does not interest us. We don't have to be concerned with SOC 1.

- SOC 2: These audits review the operational, non-financial-reporting controls of the company. THIS is what we're interested in, from an INFOSEC perspective. It covers the CIA Triad and privacy.

-- Type I: Not really all that helpful; the Type I report only validates the design of the controls at a specific moment in time.

-- Type II: THIS is the report you want. The Type II reviews the actual controls implemented in the environment, and whether they are satisfactory for the purpose, over a period of time.

- SOC 3: Not the one we want, but the one we're likely to get. The SOC 3 is a sanitized attestation that the auditor has reviewed the controls, found them satisfactory, and is affixing their stamp of approval to the audit. In this report, we don't get to see the actual controls the company is using, but we get some assurance that they exist and function properly. The company that was the target of the audit will release this wayyyy before they release the SOC 2, Type II, because the SOC 3 doesn't contain enough detail to reveal anything that could be used in a malicious attack.

NIST SP 800-37

This document is the NIST guide for applying the Risk Management Framework (RMF) to federal government IT systems in the United States. Colloquially, it just basically *is* the RMF, and may be referred to as such. The RMF replaced the practice of certification/accreditation of IT systems, which didn't involve sufficient continual monitoring and supervision.
http://nvlpubs.nist.gov/nistpubs/SpecialPublicat ions/NIST.SP.800-37r1.pdf
(For those who care, although it probably won't be on the test, the RMF superseded the old NIACAP/DIACAP/DITSCAP regulations for federal and military organizations.)

NIST SP 800-53

This NIST publication is for choosing security controls to protect IT systems. Again, it's designed for federal agencies, to make them compliant with FISMA (the Federal Information Systems Management Act, which includes strong security content), but is easily adaptable for private enterprise. It's got an exhaustive list of generic security controls and techniques (that is, it doesn't list specific vendors or products).
http://nvlpubs.nist.gov/nistpubs/SpecialPublications/NIST.SP.800-53r4.pdf

NIST FIPS 140-2

This is the NIST list of approved vendors/products that meet the requirements of cryptographic modules. Products on this list have made it through the rigorous FIPS 140-2 certification process.
http://csrc.nist.gov/groups/STM/cmvp/documents/140-1/140val-all.htm

ISO 27001

The entire 27XXX family of ISO standards deal with the practice of securing information assets, and 27001 is the foundational document. It deals with the overall Information Security Management System (ISMS)-- what Americans would call an organization's security program: the policy, processes, people, and tools involved in IT security inside an organization.

As with all ISO standards, it is comprehensive and detailed, and widely recognized around the world...and expensive: currently about $115 per copy of the document, and anywhere from $10,000 to $50,000 to get the initial certification for a medium-sized business, with another $10,000-$20,000 per year afterward for maintenance fees.

http://www.iso.org/iso/iso27001

SANS

SANS is a certification and training organization for IT security, recognized throughout the field. They also publish the Critical Security Controls list, colloquially known as the Top 20. While not expressly crafted as an implementation standard, the Top 20 is sufficiently adequate for adoption in an organization's governance to provide evidence of due diligence.

While you are required to register in order to receive the Controls document, it is free of charge.

https://www.sans.org/critical-security-controls

Cloud Security Alliance (CSA)

The CSA is an industry group of IT and security professionals with a great deal of insight into the area of cloud computing. They are at the forefront of several efforts to standardize and certify cloud implementations. You should know two particular things about the CSA:

- The Cloud Controls Matrix. A controls framework designed for cloud computing providers. Meshes well with other INFOSEC frameworks, such as ISO 27001/27002, COBIT, PCI, and NIST guidance.

- The Security, Trust, and Assurance Registry (STAR) program. CSA has created a voluntary certification regimen for cloud providers. There are three STAR tiers, with 1 being the lowest, requiring only self-certification, and 3 denoting continual monitoring.

eDiscovery

In the legal realm, the term "discovery" is the concept of finding and disclosing any information that might constitute evidence. Discovery can be used to gather evidence for either criminal or civil proceedings. For instance, when an organization receives a warrant or subpoena from a regulator/law enforcement entity to disclose any information pertaining to X, or when the organization receives notice from a plaintiff that the organization is being sued for X, the organization must, by law, go through all its data, locate material pertaining to X, and deliver it to the agency/plaintiff. Failure to disclose evidence is a crime, even if done inadvertently, and the penalties are much higher if it can be demonstrated that the organization failed to disclose evidence on purpose.

The process of ediscovery begins even before the investigation/lawsuit commences; as soon as the organization receives notice that an investigation or lawsuit is pending (that is, before receiving a warrant or subpoena), the organization must begin preparations for ediscovery. This notice is called many things: cease destruction notice, records retention notice, litigation hold notice, legal hold, and similar terms. When the organization is so notified, it must stop all data destruction activities throughout the organization. *This includes all data destruction requirements stipulated by regulation, internal policy, or other laws.* For the duration of the prosecution/litigation, the federal rules of evidence, as dictated by Congress, superseded all other directives, and the organization can't destroy any data. Destroying data that is or could be considered evidence is called *spoilage*, and is a crime as well.

The activities involved in ediscovery can include other specialized techniques and tasks, such as data forensics, asset inventory and identification, and evidence collection. These often require the services of a specialist in these areas, as most organizations don't have these people on staff on a regular basis.

eDiscovery efforts can be further complicated in a cloud environment, where the organization (as a cloud customer) does not even have physical access to the machines holding the customer's data, so locating and identifying pertinent material may be difficult. Moreover, potential evidence stored in virtualized environments (such as with cloud computing) can also be difficult to find, because virtual images are stored as files, and their contents may be hard to search while the virtual instances are not active. On top of that, cryptography is often employed in managed cloud services for security purposes, and ediscovery efforts might be stifled by encrypted data.

Another aspect of ediscovery in the cloud that may be of concern to cloud customers is the possibility of an organization's data being seized from the cloud provider because a law enforcement agency or litigant is looking for a *different* customer's data, and the two data sets just happen to be collocated on the same device. This is another reason encryption is so popular in the cloud: it protects against possible inadvertent disclosures in multitenant environments.

Chapter 4: Personnel and Training

We have to be concerned about the wetware in our environment, as well. People comprise some of our greatest risks, as well as serving as intrusion detection systems and incident response assets. Personnel Security cannot be overlooked when we design our security program.

Personnel Security efforts begin before someone even enters our environment:

- Job descriptions: Hiring managers have to work together with the HR office to craft accurate and comprehensive job descriptions for each new hire. This will be useful for several reasons, not the least of which is the liability that can be assigned to that person if management has to take punitive action against them for failing in their duties later.

- Background checks: Verifying and validating assertions a potential new hire has made on their resume is simple due diligence.

During employment, we have obligations and opportunities regarding the employee, as well:

Right to expectation of privacy: The courts have repeatedly found that surveillance is allowed in the workplace; employers are allowed to track employee behavior, especially on assets owned by the employer (phones, IT systems, etc.). However, there are limits, particularly in the realm of video monitoring, for which the employee has an expectation of privacy. These include restrooms and break areas. Moreover, everyone entering an area that is subject to video surveillance must be made aware the monitoring is happening (usually with posted notice). For other types of surveillance, it is good practice to include notice in an Acceptable Use Policy, and have employees sign the AUP.

Of course, an employee who is about to be not an employee poses certain risks, as well.

- Employees who quit: We need to recover all property owned by the organization, including keys (both crypto and physical), badges, PDAs/phones/tablets/computers, etc. A formal outbriefing is required, to remind the person of their obligations and rights regarding their relationship with the organization, and their duties regarding confidential information and ethical behavior. Shutting down their accounts (*not* deleting them, in case we need to harvest information from them), including email and voicemail. Changing access control variables that they might have shared if they were in a certain group (for instance, if there is a password used by all sysadmins, and the person leaving was in that role). Depending on the needs of the organization and the employment contract, the organization may want to pay the person leaving for any time remaining on the contract instead of remaining inside the facility and on the network.

- Terminating employees: All the same actions performed with someone leaving voluntarily, with the possible additional safeguards of having the person escorted from the facility, and performing the actions in advance of notifying the employee.

Training

[Note: the following section may contain a bit more detail than is necessary for the exam, so you can skim it. But I'm a trainer, so I probably went a bit overboard on this section.]

Personnel who are knowledgeable of the organization's policies, security risks, and their own job duties will perform better and act as another layer in your defense-in-depth security program. Obviously, as a trainer, I am biased toward stressing the important of training; realistically, because both training and security are not profit centers unless your organization specializes in those fields, those areas will be the first to face reduced budgets in times of economic hardship. But the following are a list of good training practices which might be referenced on the exam:

- Ensure that senior management endorses and supports the training program. That includes senior managers participating in all required training.

- Perform different training sessions based on the needs of the personnel involved. Your program should include:

-- Initial training: Training the employee receives when first joining the organization. The employee should not get access to IT assets in the organization until completing training, demonstrating an understanding of the material, and signing the AUP.

-- Recurring training: Training all personnel are required to take on a regular basis, such as annually.

-- Refresher training: Training required when an employee returns to the organization from an extended break, or possibly when the employee has demonstrated a lack of understanding about the security and use policies (such as when they violate the policy/procedures).

- Create a cooperative approach: In many organizations, the security office is perceived as adversarial to operations; it's the security policy that inhibits efficiency, the security office that prohibits modifications to the network, the security team that surveils behavior, etc. This relationship can actually reduce overall security posture by creating an atmosphere of fear and mistrust: if users make mistakes and may suffer punishment for them, those users will be reluctant to bring mistakes to the attention of the security office-- in fact, users might hide mistakes and find ways around security protocols if the security office is seen as too inhibitive. Instead, cultivate a relationship based on mutual trust and assistance. If the security office can co-opt users, users become another layer in our defense-in-depth. Training is a big part of this: it's usually the first time new users will encounter personnel from the security office and be exposed to the organization's security policy. Friendliness and approachability will foment much better results than fear and threat of punishment. Some methods for accomplishing this:

-- Handouts. Little giveaways go a long way. Pens, notepads, coffee mugs, T-shirts with the INFOSEC office's logo and contact info are all great ways to increase affinity and decrease animosity with the operational personnel.

- FOOD. Offering snacks/meals at security training events is an outstanding way to ensure attendance and create goodwill throughout the organization.

- Personalization. If you can cater to the needs of specific personnel, that will enhance their reception of the information you're delivering. Carry this a step forward, too: offer informative, voluntary sessions scheduled during free time (lunch breaks, before or after work) in which you provide security tips and hints that users can utilize in their personal life; a class titled, "Securing Your Home Network" will be attended by more people than any mandatory annual training session.

- EXPLAIN. People are much more inclined to conform to policy if they understand the reasons behind it. This is also a great opportunity to share anecdotes and tales of security breaches experienced by competitors/colleagues in the field, which often stick in memory much better than academic concepts.

Awareness

Awareness efforts, as distinct from training or education, are intended to continually reinforce users' understanding and regard for security concerns. The cliched awareness "program" is a set of posters warning about the dangers of hackers and malware and whatnot.

Training Day
Traditionally, education, training, and awareness are distinguished by level of formality and intensity. Education is largely the province of academic venues-- colleges and universities. Training is usually delivered by members of the industry and subject matter experts. Awareness is usually performed by inanimate objects. For purposes of the exam, treat them synonymously (except for the thing about the posters-- posters are always about awareness).

Chapter 5: Tech

Some INFOSEC tests lean more heavily to the techie side than others. For instance, Network+ and Security+ will have more explicit questions about the bits and bytes than the CISA or CISSP; the CompTIA stuff is more for admins and will contain technical material and the ISACA/ISC2 stuff is more for security practitioners and is heavy into governance. I am NOT a wirehead, so this portion is never my strong suit. However, it is possible to understand the substance and pass the test(s) without being an engineer.

Networking Infrastructure

Communication is data moving over a medium. For IT networking, that could be wiring, fiber optics, or wireless transmission. Here's what you need to know for the exam:

Twisted pair: Two strands of copper wire rolled around each other. Modern Ethernet networks use Category 6 (Cat 6) twisted pair bundled cables.

Fiber: Fiber optics are spun-glass lines that can carry more data faster than copper. More expensive and complicated than wire.

Wireless: Data transmission without physical connections, usually using radio waves. Requires a wireless interface capability in the sending machine, and a wireless access point on the network.

NIC: A network interface controller allows a computer to link to a network. Each NIC on a machine must be assigned its own media access control address

(MAC address), even if multiple NICs are inside a single machine.

IPSec: Okay, this isn't infrastructure, it's a secure networking protocol, but I'm not sure where else to put it, because this book doesn't have a "secure protocols" section...so I'm sticking it here. What you need to know about IPSec is this: in its default, out-of-the-box configuration, IPSec will drop any communication initiated with another machine that does not have IPSec. Let me put that another way, because it's worth remembering: if your machine has IPSec, it won't talk to any machines that don't have IPSec, unless you tell it to do so. So...bear that in mind.

Network topology

You may be asked some questions about rudimentary network design concepts. Know these topologies:

- Bus: All devices are connected to a main trunk line. Least expensive option, but with the greatest chance for disruption, because everything is along a single point of failure.

- Star: All devices are linked through a central point. Inexpensive, but a single point of failure remains at that center.

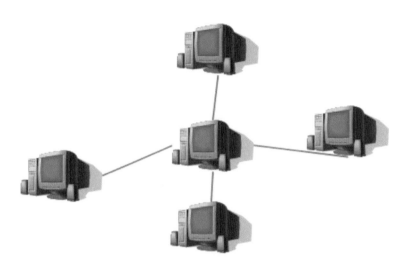

- Mesh: All devices have direct connections to all other devices. Most expensive, because look at all that cable. Also a pain to administer. But least chance of disruption, because there are no single points of failure.

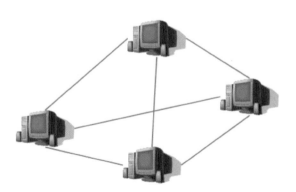

- Ring: Each device is connected to two other devices, and traffic is passed around the loop. Not the same as a bus, because the devices connect to each other instead of a trunk. Still susceptible to numerous points of failure, but not expensive.

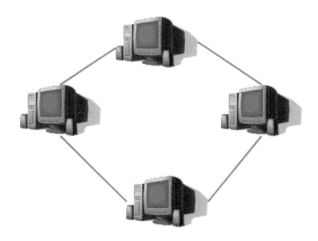

Shut Up.
Do not mock my awesome artwork skills.

Network Communications

Ports

Machines on a network communicate via a number of logical "ports"; each port is a notional location through which electronic information passes according to type and configuration. The rules for how information should be structured are called "protocols"; most protocols are associated with a certain kind of communication, and are assigned a specific port for that particular kind of traffic.

There are 65,535 possible distinct ports in common electronic communication. This overall collection is split into three named sets:

"Well-known" ports: Ports 0 to 1023 are the "well-known" ports; yes, they are well known, but that is also the named of that group of ports. Because IT nerds are very creative people. The well-known ports include protocols and services that are ubiquitous in the field, such as FTP, HTTP, telnet, and the like.

"Registered" ports: Ports 1024 to 49,151. These are usually assigned to IT vendors looking to map a product with a new service to a port that is not otherwise in use. Examples include Docker, BitTorrent, and many online games.

"Dynamic" ports: Ports 49,152 to 65,535. These can't be reserved for a particular use, and instead are utilized for specific private purposes, often temporarily or strictly internally.

A list of ports to memorize:

80	HTTP
20-21	FTP
22	SSH
23	Telnet
25	SMTP
118	SQL services
161	SNMP
194	IRC
443	HTTPS
500	ISAMP/IKE

Note: Not all of the exams will ask you about specific ports numbers/services; of the many INFOSEC tests, expect the Network+ and Security+ exams to contain the most questions of this type.

The TCP/IP Handshake

In network communications using the TCP/IP protocol suite, the participants in a given conversation (also called a "session") start by setting things up; this is called the "TCP/IP handshake," or the "three-way handshake." It's a three-step process, and looks like this:

The first machine sends a SYN packet (for "synchronize") to the other machine.

The second machine receives the SYN packet and replies with a SYN/ACK packet (for "synchronize/acknowledge").

The first machine responds with an ACK packet.

The session is now created, and the conversation can begin. The machines might exchange more protocol-based communications to establish some other parameters (for instance, if they are going to use encryption, they'll have to exchange information about which cryptosystems and key lengths they'll agree to utilize for the session) before the actual data, the meat of the conversation, is sent back and forth.

The handshake looks like this:

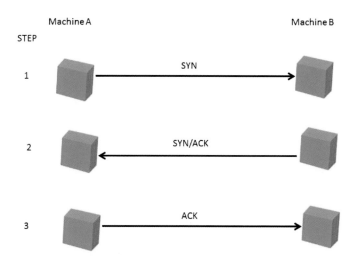

Attacks That Abuse the TCP/IP Handshake

Because the TCP/IP handshake is used so extensively in online communications, it is a tool that can be leveraged for malicious purposes, as well. Attackers have been using techniques based on the handshake for decades, but some of them are still in use today: in 2016, the highest-rate DDOS attacks to date [600 Gb/s and 1.2 Tb/s] struck targets using these (and other) methods.

As they sometimes show up in exam questions, they are worth knowing by name and specific technique.

> - SYN flood: Just like it sounds; the attacker inundates the target machine with a vast number of SYN packets from various attack machines (the 'bots in the 'botnet), forcing the target to try to reply to all of them, overwhelming it.

> - ACK flood: The same thing, but with ACK packets, meant to overwhelm the target device by forcing it to check for sessions that were never actually created.

> - SYN spoofing: A variant of the SYN attack. The attacker will choose a robust third party, perhaps even a cloud provider, and launch a vast number of SYN packets, often from a 'botnet, but all with a single, spoofed IP address-- the IP address is the actual target of the attack. When the third party devices respond to the SYN packets with an equal number of SYN-ACK packets, the target machine (the one with the IP address the attacker used in the spoofed packets) will be overwhelmed.

A depiction of a spoofed SYN flood.

Other Traffic-Based Attacks

You should also know these attacks, because they do come up on tests.

- Smurf attack (ping flood): Instead of using the TCP/IP handshake, the attacker uses ICMP echo-request packets (with the target's spoofed IP address) sent to a network, using the network's broadcast address. Using the broadcast address means the packets will be sent to all the machines on that network; because the ICMP packets request a response, all the machines on that network then send replies to the target (because the request was crafted with the target's spoofed address). This is very much like the spoofed SYN attack, but with a multiplier effect: instead of a few machines responding to the initial attack packets, every machine on the network will respond to every attack packet, increasing the magnitude of the attack exponentially.

- Fraggle attack: Similar to the Smurf attack, but with UDP packets.

- Teardrop attack: Sending IP packets that are designed in such a way that they overlap when they are reassembled by the target machine, overwhelming and crashing it.

- Ping of Death: Sending an ICMP echo-request (ping) packet that is designed in such a way that it causes a buffer overflow in the target machine.

Network Boundaries

We can view networks as distinct entities, even though --in all likelihood-- they're connected, because they wouldn't be of much use if they weren't. So we often treat the network of devices that belong to our organization and under our control as internal, and all other devices and media as outside our perimeter. Generally, we want to protect the things inside much more than the things outside...mainly because we can and we can't, respectively.

The boundary between our internal network and the outside world (where it connects with the Intercybernetwebs) is where we take a lot of care to set various controls, because that's the point where data could escape our control and where aggressors can get in. If data is lost inside our perimeter, that is usually less troublesome and costly. So the devices that sit between the outside world and our sweet, sweet internal network must be hardened and protected with a care and manner more intense than many of our other resources.

Some terms and concepts to bear in mind for the exam:

DMZ (ostensibly named for "demilitarized zone," like in warfare, but nobody ever calls it that): The buffer area between the Internet and our internal network; we still own the resources inside the DMZ, and they are technically part of our network, but we treat devices at these boundaries differently than other internal resources.

Bastion hosts: Refers to hardened boxes, including and often describing devices in the DMZ. Bastion hosts will have less functionality than devices of similar design and capability, because we strip away anything other than the bare minimum necessary for the device to accomplish its specific task; the less functionality a box has, the more secure it becomes. With bastion hosts, we remove all default accounts, all guest accounts, all superfluous services, and any software libraries not particularly needed; we close all ports except for those required for the intended type of traffic through that box; and we may add extra layers of access controls and security logging.

Firewall: A device that filters information between networks. Often placed in the DMZ, between the outside world and the internal network. Firewalls come in different flavors, and the exam might have questions about when to employ specific types of firewalls, or which ones will serve a given purpose better than others. These are the things you should know about firewalls:

- Proxy server: A type of firewall that acts on the behalf of a machine in one network, displaying information from another network. This obscures the identification of machines inside the organization from anyone outside it. It can also serve the purpose of filtering content based on URLs or domains.

- Packet filtering: The firewall drops traffic packets based on information within the packets, such as the source or destination addresses, which ports they were intended to traverse, or the protocols under which the packet was designed.

- Stateful inspection: A firewall capability where the device can recognize known, active connections and eliminates any traffic packets that couldn't possibly be part of these authorized communications, based on the configuration or nature of the packets themselves. Also known as "dynamic packet filtering."

- Application-layer: Firewalls that operate on the application layer can understand given protocols, and can therefore identify corrupt or tainted packets that are designed to bypass other security measures.

> **Just because**
> IDS/IPS assets can be placed on individual machines or on connections between machines; these are called host-based and network-based (HIDS and NIDS), respectively.

Intrusion detection/prevention systems (IDS/IPS): Assets that recognize malicious traffics or access attempts; can be hardware or software or both. The main difference between IDSs and IPSs is that an IDS is a fairly passive system which only logs such traffic and sends an alert to the office or personnel tasked with reviewing these things, while an IPS can take an active role in security by taking measures to deter identified malicious traffic, often by closing ports (and an IPS usually also functions as an IDS, with the alerting and tracking and whatnot).

Remote Access

Networks become even more useful when users can communicate with them without being directly connected or present at the same site as the network itself. We call this "remote access": users connecting to the network, and operating on it as if they were present.

These are the things you need to know about remote access:

- Authentication, Authorization, and Accounting (AAA) Protocols. Establish connections for remote users, and provide some mechanism for trusted authentication.

-- RADIUS: An early remote connection protocol still in use; utilizes TCP or UDP. Encrypts only passwords; username is sent in the clear

-- Diameter: A protocol devised to replace RADIUS; however, they are both still in use, usually for different purposes. Uses TCP or SCTP.

-- TACACS+: Utilizes TCP; all connection content (username and password) is encrypted.

- Authentication Schemes. The mechanisms and/formats often used by AAA protocols.

-- PPP: Point-To-Point protocol. A protocol for creating a connection directly between two nodes in a network.

-- PAP: Password Authentication Protocol. Used in PPP; transmits passwords over the network in the clear, so cannot be considered secure.

-- CHAP: Challenge-Authentication Handshake Protocol. Offers protection against replay attacks. The Microsoft version, MS-CHAP, has been cracked.

-- EAP: Extensible Authentication Protocol. Designed as an authentication extension to PPP. A message format framework frequently used in wireless and point-to-point connections.

- Virtual Private Network (VPN). A method of remote access that creates a temporary "tunnel" between the remote user and the network, where the packets of one network are recognized by and used on another network.

-- L2TP: Layer 2 Tunneling Protocol. Does not inherently provide the authentication or confidentiality, but is often combined with an encryption protocol that does (such as IPSEC).

-- PPTP: Microsoft's tunneling protocol, now obsolete, due to many security vulnerabilities.

Malware

Malicious software will be a constant threat, to greater or lesser degree, for all organizations, perpetually. A broad definition of malware would encompass several traits:

Software that:

- Performs functions unintended by the user.

- Affects the optimal operation of the system.

- Gathers and exports data without the user's knowledge.

- Protects itself from simple removal.

- Escalates its own privileges.

- Costs the user money.

Here's what you need to know about malware for the test:

- Worms: Self-replicating applets that don't usually have a "payload"-- they don't usually form another kind of attack other than hogging bandwidth and processing capacity. This does not mean they are benign or harmless, though. Worms usually don't need any other software or substance to perform their activity.

Mal Where?
I don't think I'm the first to point out that the standard definitions of malware can usually be applied to most anti-malware applications and vendors.

- Viruses: Usually, a piece of malware that attaches itself to another program/object in order to perform its activity. Sometimes includes functions that allow it to perform additional deleterious actions once it is admitted to the environment. Usually not self-replicating; often needs some other object or function in order to activate and replicate, thus distinguishing viruses from worms.

- Trojan horse applications: A means of delivering malware. The user executes/installs a certain piece of software purposefully, but that software also includes something malicious.

- Rootkits: Malware that gives the attacker root-level access to the target machine.

- Zero-day exploits: Not necessarily a malware vector, but usually included in the discussion of malware. A vulnerability that exists but is not widely known, or known only to the attacker.

- Ransomware: The practice of infiltrating an IT environment, finding valuable data or endpoints, encrypting them with a powerful cryptosystem, and then demanding payment for the crypto keys. This is extortion (or, more accurately, data-napping) using cryptography and hacking. It may or may not be facilitated with malware, but is often discussed along with that topic.

- Zombies: Machines that have been infected by an unauthorized remote user, and can be operated by this attacker, often for purposes of attacking other targets.

- 'botnets: Groups of zombied machines, often used as rented platforms for DDOS attacks or for distributed computing tasks.

Cloud Computing

Cloud computing is the notion of having data processing and storage performed at a centralized, administered location while users and operations are not in the same location, but can connect via the Internet. When we discuss cloud computing in terms of

the exam, we're using talking about cloud providers--
those vendors that sell cloud services. And we're
usually talking about public cloud providers...but let's
start with some definitions.

The NIST definition: This is pretty much the
gold standard in the industry, and accepted as the
formal definition of what cloud computing is. A cloud
computing solution must include:

- Metered service. Customers pay according to
a pre-negotiated fee structure (could be per-use, per-
user, per-bandwidth, per-minute, per-Gb, etc.).

- Rapid elasticity. When customers need more
capacity, the cloud can escalate to meet those needs;
when usage requirements decline, customers are not
charged for the infrequent, higher rate of usage.
Another way to think of it would be "instant
scalability."

- Broad network access. Customers can reach
the cloud provider from anywhere they can get Internet
access, and the cloud provider is set up for appropriate
bandwidth provision to make the connection and usage
efficient.

- On-demand self-service. Customers choose
how and when they use the cloud, without needing to
interact individually with the cloud provider every time
they need access or to add more functionality.

- Resource pooling. This is why cloud
operations represent a chance to reduce costs for
customers, but also profitability for providers. Cloud
providers can purchase a wide array and high quantity

of devices and personnel with IT-centric skillsets, and offer these things to cloud customers at a much lower cost than the customer would have to expend to purchase an equitable number of devices and staff to achieve the functionality. How is this done? Cloud customers can share a lot of the infrastructure in the cloud solution, using only fractional or momentary capacity, whereas the customer cannot purchase only a fraction of a device if they want to use it within their own environment; the customer would have to contend with unused capacity (which has been paid for but yields no revenue) or only have the minimum level of infrastructure to provide a constant maximum usage (with no potential for scalability, and constant threat of falling below that threshold for any outages). Virtualization is an essential ingredient in allowing for resource pooling, and that is discussed later in this section.

Memorize those five traits. Not all the text describing them, but the characteristics themselves. You can find the original NIST doc here: http://nvlpubs.nist.gov/nistpubs/Legacy/SP/nistspecialp ublication800-145.pdf

Other vital information/definitions to know, in terms of cloud computing:

Private cloud: A centralized data center owned by your organization, which is solely responsible for administration and all costs, and only accessed by that organization's customers and users. The academic definition of public cloud may differ from common understanding of the term; that is, some people think of a "private cloud" solution as purchasing/leasing a specific network segment or set of hardware from a cloud provider. This is **NOT** a private cloud in terms of the exam. Here's the best way to reconcile the difference when you're taking the test: if the organization using the cloud environment owns the actual hardware -the hosts, the servers, the routers and switches- then that *is* a private cloud; if the organization using the cloud environment is renting/leasing these things from another company, that is *not* a private cloud (that's a private space in a public cloud).

Public cloud: When cloud services are offered to the public, and anyone can pay for them, that is a public cloud. Major public cloud providers include Amazon Web Services (AWS), Azure (Microsoft), and RackSpace. We are usually talking about public cloud services when discussing cloud computing on the tests.

Community cloud: Not public, not private; usage and ownership are limited to a specific group, usually including a set of people or organizations that have some shared affinity. A good example might be online gaming entities such as PlayStation Network; while Sony might own some of the administrative tools, computing and storage might be distributed throughout the user community, or might be hosted by a certain game company's data center; only the stakeholders have access and responsibility (stakeholders might include the gamers who subscribe to the service, Sony, the game company, etc.).

Hybrid cloud: Some combination of private, public, and/or community cloud configurations.

Infrastructure-as-a-Service (IaaS): A bare-bones cloud offering; the cloud provider will have a data center that contains the necessary hardware and utilities and communication capability, but that's it. The cloud customer will have to install an OS (or OSs) and whatever software the customer deems necessary, and the customer will be responsible for administration of these things. IaaS configurations are often good for BC/DR purposes (as a hot/warm site).

Platform-as-a-Service (PaaS): The cloud provider offers not only everything in the IaaS, but also an OS; the cloud customer installs their own software. PaaS configurations are often good for software development purposes.

Software-as-a-Service (SaaS): The most comprehensive of cloud offerings. The cloud provider supplies everything included in IaaS and PaaS configurations, as well as applications on top of the OS. Think: Office 365 or MMORPGs.

Virtualization: Software that pretends to be a total build of a new computer. Many virtual machines (VMs) can ride on a single host computer, and can be operated without affecting each other, which allows for widespread scaling of the environment (say, 20 hosts might run 400 VMs, so 400 different users can run their own "computer" simultaneously, without interfering with each other, or even knowing each other exist). VMs are what make cloud services financially viable: a cloud data center can spread the costs of a massive data center over many more users than a single enterprise would be able to contain with the same amount of investment. When several cloud customers have users that share VMs hosts within the provider's data center, we call this the **multi-tenant**

environment. This brings its own risks in addition to the benefits; I'll address those later in this chapter.

The Hypervisor: The interface between a VM and its host computer. Hypervisors come in two flavors:

> - Type I: Rides on the hardware of the host system; known as a "bare metal hypervisor."
>
> - Type II: Run from the OS of the host, so it's an OS on an OS.

Yeah, go ahead and memorize those. Sorry.

<u>Hyperactive</u>
The exams are going with the assumption that attackers would prefer to hack a Type II hypervisor, because there is more attack surface on software than hardware. Never having been a criminal, I can't say whether that assumption has any validity, but it's a question they might ask on a test, so go ahead and memorize that, too.

A VM is *not* an emulator. And emulator is software that allows you to run a program in a non-native environment; a VM runs an entire OS, as if the OS was on its own machine. Emulators are usually deployed for very specific, limited uses, such as playing old DOS or Apple IIe games on modern Windows machines.

Software-Defined Networking (SDN): Another important technology that promotes the efficacy of cloud computing; instead of using physical connections to form networks and subnets, SDN allows network architects and engineers to maintain basic physical connections in a data center, but then customize the logical network map such that new subnets and network segments can be created and modified from a centralized control interface (a piece of software, hence the name). The very, very important thing to remember when you're taking the test is that any organization using SDN solutions must be extremely careful about protecting that centralized controller, and all the elements of the SDN which can govern the actual devices on the network-- this is called the management plane, or the control plane, and that plane must have separate access and distinct controls so that it can't be misused and users can't overreach their own permissions and fiddle with the network.

Physical cloud data center design: Wait-- "cloud physical data center design"? Or maybe "cloud data center physical design"? Whatever-- the way you should construct a data center, in terms of actual facility functions, if you're going to be a cloud provider. Like, architecture and engineering and stuff. What you want to do (before taking your exam) is get familiar with the Uptime Institute's tier certifications: https://en.wikipedia.org/wiki/Uptime_Institute#Tier_ce rtifications. There are four of them. Know that Tier 1 is the lowest, and Tier 4 is the highest, and that the Uptime Institute is measuring data centers in terms of robustness and redundancy, for *everything*-- that includes, power, bandwidth, comms, HVAC, services to personnel...anything that could affect the smooth and constant operation of a data center.

Software

There will be a great many questions about software security, design, testing, and usage on the exam. The next few subsections will cover those things related to software that may show up on various tests.

Databases

There may be a lot of questions about databases on your exam; without going into too much detail, I'm going to cover some database basics, and then a very brief discussion of some database security concepts.

A database is a structured software solution that allows information to be arranged in a specific way so that it can be accessed and cross-referenced. The most common form of modern database is known as "relational": all data in the data set are arranged in some way that relates each element to other elements.

For instance, think of information arranged in a table. Say, it's information about pet dogs.

Chip #	Name	Breed	Weight (lbs)	Color	Cuteness Factor
12345678	Rex	Chihuahua	3	Tan	Not Cute
23456789	Polly	Poodle	36	White	Cute
34567890	Jake	Mutt	70	Yellow	Very Cute
45678901	Dudley	Bassett	45	Brown	Very Cute

The information in the table is arranged such that certain traits, called *attributes*, are assigned to each individual subject (in this case, each subject is a specific dog). The attributes are labeled in that top line, and all the information of a certain type is contained in that column, for each specific dog. Each row specifies an individual, unique dog, and is called a *tuple*. Each tuple needs a *primary key*; that unique identifier for that subject. In this table, the primary key is the RFID chip implanted in each dog; every chip has a unique number that will never be repeated for another dog. If we tried to use other attributes for the primary key (like, say, the dog's name), it wouldn't work, because there might be more than one dog with the same name.

Each box that can contain data is called a *field*; the field is an intersection between a column and a row, and can be assigned an address in that way, for easier lookup and retrieval later. The primary key field must always have a value. The others fields don't necessarily need to have values assigned (for instance, we might not know the weight of a given dog, or it might not have a name).

Attributes can have various data types, which are assigned by the data owner and database administrator. For instance, in this table, the Weight attribute is numerical, and the Cuteness Factor is a dropdown box of four choices: "Not Cute," "Cute," "Very Cute," and "Undetermined" (I didn't show the dropdown box, but you can see the relevant fields, as populated with demo data).

My dog, Jake, is the cutest, even though there is no option in the sample table to demonstrate that:

Databases will have multiple tables, often with attributes and fields populated from data in other tables within that same database. For instance, we might have another table that shows information about the dogs' diet.

Dog	Food	Feeding Time	Amount (cups)
34567890	Kibble	every 12 hours	2
12345678	Wet	morning	.5

In this case, the primary key (often the first column/attribute in the table) is the same as in our other table. Sometimes, the primary key for a table is used as just a simple attribute in another table; in that case, it's called a *foreign key* (in the table where it's not the primary).

The real power of databases comes from the way we can elicit information from them; we can questions about the data set, and the results can enhance our operational capabilities. For instance, we can ask the database, "How much kibble do we need for all our dogs?" the result will be a discrete amount based on all Amount attributes added up for those tuples that have Food as Kibble (ignoring the tuples with Food as Wet). These results are often called *reports*, and the questions we ask are called *queries*; database queries are structured as a form of arithmetic (Boolean) logic. With the right kind of queries, we can gain powerful insight into operations through the database; we might learn how much food has been purchased in the last three months, how to predict food usage based on breed, or when we can save money by buying in bulk.

There are other kinds of databases, such as the hierarchical and network types, which were precursors to the relational model, and the object-oriented databases and JSON communication standard for sending database information over networks, which came later.

A database management system (DBMS) is the program that collects data into databases, allows queries, reports, and user views, and interacts with users, administrators and other programs. In regular practice, when we refer to a "database," we're usually talking about a DBMS. Common DBMSs include MySQL, Oracle, and Microsoft SQL Server.

You should be familiar with this basic information about databases for the exam. You also need to know the following pertinent knowledge about how to secure databases.

Databases can sometimes be corrupted or confused by erroneous data that does not fit properly into specific fields. For instance, if a database expects a field to contain information limited to a few characters, and instead a string of 10,000 characters are entered, the program might hang or crash, or the data might be saved in the wrong storage location, and might allow the user entering the overly-long string to access other data within the database. This is usually referred to as a *buffer overflow*; buffers are short-term caches of data most often used for temporary processing, and putting more information into a buffer than it can handle can result in fail states or non-secure situations. Buffer overflows used to be popular and successful means of attacking software (and, in many cases, still are).

Another way to attack a database is to enter information the database can't use to perform its normal operation. For instance, using our Dog Database example, the Weight attribute is for numeric data; if a user enters a string of alphabetic characters instead, any calculations the database performs using the Weight field are going to throw off if the database tries to use letters instead of numbers (example: the equation, "Food divided by Weight" is going to fail if the database tries to calculate, "70/Noodle").

Finally, another extremely popular way to attack a database is to enter administrative commands into fields, in an attempt to trick the database software into running the command as an execution, leaving the (malicious) user with administrative access or some other unauthorized permission. This is usually referred to as *SQL Injection*, and is very common.

All of these attacks --buffer overflow, erroneous data, and SQL injection-- are listed by OWASP in their list of Top Ten security risks for Web applications every time the list is published (usually every other year). The names of the attacks might vary, and their position on the list might fluctuate, but they boil down to these three kinds of attacks.

OWASP is the Open Web Application Security Project, an online group of software and security practitioners that seek to create a more secure Internet environment. Basically, it's a Wiki with a lot of great data and tools for securing Web programs and data. Know this for the test.

REST/SOAP: Another aspect of Internet communication you'll have to know about for the test is how to access Web services. Currently, there are two main motifs for coordinating this function: REST and SOAP. I wish I could explain the differences between the two, but I barely understand the notion myself. I'd suggest you look here, at this essay, which does a much better job than I ever could: http://blog.smartbear.com/apis/understanding-soap-and-rest-basics/.

Here's the only help I can offer, instead: if the question on the exam mentions JSON, then it's about REST; if it mentions XML, then it's usually about SOAP. That's all I've got.

The SDLC

The exams will contain questions about the SDLC; the process of creating, testing, and implementing new acquisitions. Depending on the context, the abbreviation might stand for "system development life cycle" or "software development life cycle." Either way, it pertains to acquisition of IT assets, either by purchase from an external vendor or internal design for a specific purpose.

Whatever the usage, the SDLC is usually defined as a multi-stage process, which includes elements along the lines of:

- Definitions of requirements: The pre-design phase, where the organization determines just what the purpose of the system will be, from a business standpoint-- that is, an operational perspective. The sponsor of the new system (the office funding the purchase, which is also usually the department that is going to be using it in production) lays out the actual needs the system is intended to fulfill: the business case for the system. This is usually done in a committee of some sort, with input from various stakeholders (which might include representatives from the gaining organization's IT department, security office, user community --specifically, the users who are going to be most likely to use the new system-- and the department making the purchase, as well as any other entity within the organization that might be affected by the new acquisition).

   - Analysis: In this step, the committee, with strong influence from the department funding the acquisition, will determine the best approach to fulfilling the needs described in the prior phase. The group will decide which option is best: purchasing an existing system from a known vendor, crafting a request for bids for a custom-built system, or designing and building a new system internally (if the organization has a system-development capability). The group will perform cost-benefit analyses of potential tradeoffs, and determine how the new acquisition will fit into the existing environment. In some cases, when the department making the purchase already knows what they want, and has chosen to purchases a commercial product, and identified that product in the earlier phase of the SDLC, this phase can be attenuated or modified.

   - Design: Just like it sounds. If the system is going to be purchased from a vendor, representatives from the gaining organization will work with the vendor to determine how the product needs to be configured to work best in the organization's environment. If the system is being created by the organization itself, engineers will work with the stakeholders to determine how best to meet the needs identified in the first phase of the SDLC.

- Creation: The thing is purchased or built.

- Testing: In this phase, the system is tested to determine whether it meets the functional and non-functional requirements of the organization. The functional requirements are those business needs identified in the first phase of the SDLC: in other words, what the system is expected to *do*. The non-functional requirements are everything else: size, color, shape, etc. More in-depth discussion of testing follows a little later in this chapter.

Here's a gimme
Security is almost always a *non-functional* requirement. Security is not part of operations; it supports operations. The exception would be in the case of security products, where security is actually the purpose of the system. That's a question that often shows up on exams.

- Implementation: The new system is moved into the production environment. This is done carefully and deliberately, with the understanding that any conflicts that arise (for instance, if the system adversely affects the existing environment in a way that testing did not reveal) might force the entire process back at least one phase in the SDLC. Training and familiarization for the users who will be using the new system is usually done in this phase, as well.

- Operations and maintenance: Once the system has been put into production, the SDLC does not end; the system must be continually monitored and maintained as the environment changes over time (both in terms of threats and functions).

- Secure disposal: In some versions of the SDLC, this last phase is included as part of the overall process. When the organization is done with the system, it must be pulled out of production with the same level of deliberation used during the Implementation phase, and efforts must be made to ensure that no data is lost or affected.

In the field of system development (the actual building/programming of the hardware/software, or the Creation phase of the SDLC that was just described), there are several popular methods you should be familiar with for exam purposes. They are:

- Waterfall: Performed in sequential steps, where all the activities in a given step must be completed before moving on to the next step. This method is prescriptive and non-iterative, like a checklist. While there are different versions of the Waterfall, the traditional method looks pretty much like the overall SDLC, with phases for defining requirements, analysis, etc.

It's called the Waterfall because of how each step must be totally completed before moving on, and is often depicted this way:

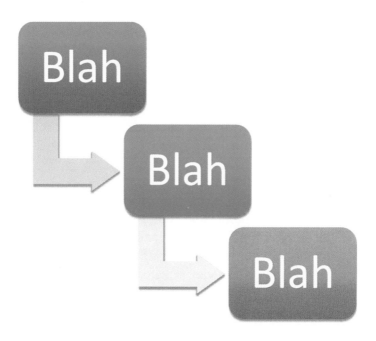

(Where "blah" is whatever title the organization has assigned to each phase of its Waterfall method.)

- Prototyping: Just like it sounds-- experimental versions of the system are created in order to determine their suitability for eventual acceptance. Usually, the prototyping model involves breaking the overall system in smaller sub-parts, and creating prototypes of each part, until they are all assembled when each one meets the needs of the customer/users. Prototyping is often combined with other methods. It's essential to include the users in the prototyping process, so that the developers can be sure the prototype and its subsequent versions are meeting user needs as the process continues. Prototyping is a fundamental aspect of other (very similar) methodologies called Rapid Application Development (RAD) and Joint Application Development (JAD), which also include the heavy influence of user input during the development process.

- Spiral: Where the Waterfall is non-iterative, the Spiral is iterative, meaning the development process involves continual repetition of steps and phases in an effort to enhance risk reduction for the end product. Each repeated phase will include a risk analysis.

- Agile: Because the older, traditional models seemed too cumbersome and micromanaged to meet the needs of modern software developers, several new methodologies were created in the 1990s to promote "lightweight" software development. *Agile* is the term associated with this family of models, which emphasizes the precepts of speed of development, iterative approaches, flexibility, and reduced reliance on formal processes. The aforementioned RAD model is in the Agile family, as are the well-known Scrum model and the "extreme programming" model (abbreviated as "XP," because there is absolutely NOTHING else in the IT world that uses the term "XP," right? <sigh>).

A Handy-Dandy Table For You To Memorize:

Model	Intended Benefits	Potential Downsides	Other
Waterfall	Bug minimization	Lack of flexibility; micromanagement	Sequential (non-iterative) process where all activities in each step must be complete before the next step starts
Prototyping	Accelerated delivery schedule; flexibility	Possible inclusion of errors	Included in RAD, JAD, and many Agile models
Spiral	Risk analysis/reduction	Delayed production	Iterative model
Agile	Flexibility; speed to production; reduced cost	Lack of documentation	Examples include Scrum and extreme programming
Scrum	Recognizes customer needs may change before system development is complete; speed	Not suitable for large systems requiring detailed testing	Characterized by continual team meetings and interchangeable developers
Extreme programming	Speed, extensive code review	Sub-teams can lose sight of overall system design; scope creep	Programming in teams of two developers; frequent partial releases
DevOps	Combines input from operational units (such as the IT department) when designing new systems	Difficult to implement in large organizations that don't have the requisite flexibility; can also lead to partial and incomplete application components.	Another child of Agile

Software Testing

Before software is put into production, it's important to test it for both functional and non-functional purposes (the latter includes security testing). There are several methods for doing so that you should be familiar with for exam purposes.

Static testing: Testing done without running the application; a review of the source code. This is often referred to as "white box" testing, because the testers see what's inside the box (the program).

Dynamic testing: Testing performed when running the program; checking outcomes to determine whether the application is performing properly. Often referred to as "black box" testing, because the testers don't see the "inside" of the program (the code), they only see the results.

"Fuzz" testing: A dynamic testing technique where massive amounts of random inputs are feed into an application in order to see if it goes into a failure state and determine how the program handles failure states.

Fault testing: A type of dynamic test where the input is purposefully incorrect/misconfigured, in order to create failure states and determine the programs response to those failure states. Simulates malicious, untrained, or unintelligent users (in other words, the average user community).

> **Whatever testing method is used, it's important to remember never to use live production data in tests. Instead, either use randomized invalid data, or obscure/anonymize production data for the purpose.**

The metric usually discussed in testing is "coverage." In code review, coverage can refer to the number of lines of the source code that are reviewed; this is often expressed as a percentage of the total number of lines in the program (so to achieve 50% coverage in a review of a million-line program would entail reviewing 500,000 lines of code). In dynamic testing, coverage represents the number of possible paths and outcomes a program might produce.

While coverage is a popular methodology, it is not exactly an accurate portrayal of a program's suitability or utility. For instance, even a 100% code review may not ensure that a program is bug-free and secure when it's delivered. Why? Several reasons. For instance, the testing team/tools might not identify all the bugs in the code, even if every line is reviewed. Also, the testers/tools can only search for known vulnerabilities; they won't be able to recognize those vulnerabilities that will eventually become zero-day exploits when someone else discovers a new hacking methodology.

Obfuscation

When live data cannot or should not be used (such as in testing, or to enforce least privilege), we can often use the practice of obfuscation to create a realistic data set that doesn't reveal any sensitive or raw data.

Testing should never be performed by the personnel/team/office that developed the software, for two reasons:

- An inherent conflict of interest

- Potential in ability to recognize faults in their product (else they would not have included those faults to begin with); it's best to get fresh eyes on software for testing purposes.

There are several obfuscation methods you should be familiar with:

- Randomization: Replacing the raw data with randomly-generated data. Might not be adequate for the testing purpose, because the random values might not truly test the application/system the same way production data would. Even if the data is randomized, it's best to try to attempt to make the obfuscated data as similar to the raw data as possible; for interest, if the original data is in the form of fields that contain numeric strings of a certain length (say, credit card numbers, or Social Security numbers), then the randomized strings should be numerical and of the same length.

- Masking: Obscuring a portion of the data, and replacing it with dummy characters. Very useful in providing least privilege; often used with credit cards and SS numbers, by only displaying the last four characters of the original fields, and replacing the rest of the data with Xs.

- Null sets: Just removing the data from the fields. Not very useful at all, for the purpose of testing.

Anonymization

In a similar vein, anonymization is the practice of attenuating the possibility of disclosing sensitive personal information from aggregation of non-sensitive material. Even though some data may not include PII, volumes of it can collected by malicious entities in order to reveal something sensitive.

For instance, demographic information could be used for hostile purposes: someone looking to target me might want to get Ben Malisow's home address, but that element of information is protected and difficult to find easily. However, they might be able to find the home address of a middle-aged man who was born in Wisconsin, went to school in Colorado, lives in New Orleans, and owns a dog; by narrowing down a field of possible similar entities, using non-sensitive information that isn't usually protected, they may be able to determine the information they're looking for.

Anonymization involves sanitizing non-sensitive information that may have secondary or tertiary effects if disclosed. Performing this function requires reviewing the data set, analyzing possible threat vectors and risks, and then either removing or masking the data so as not to reveal anything sensitive.

DLP

DLP is the term associated with solutions that provide egress monitoring; it can stand for "data loss prevention," or "data leak protection," or any combination of those words-- the abbreviation itself does not matter, only the overall concept.

DLP tools can identify sensitive data leaving the control of the data owner, and enforce policies restricting/prohibiting egress. Optimally, DLP solutions will work for any data being transported, whether it is in the form of email, attachments, ftp, removable media, or whatever else.

In order to function properly, the DLP tool must be taught which data within your organization is sensitive, and how to distinguish it from other data sets. This process could take several forms, such as:

- Definitions-based: You can instruct the DLP tool how to identify sensitive assets by defining characteristics unique to those data sets. For instance, if you want to reduce the possibility of disclosing credit card data, you would define the controlled data as any string of numerical characters 12-19 characters long, possibly separated by dashes.

- Label-based: The DLP tool might look for particular labels assigned to particular files. This requires a disciplined, formalized approach to labeling, which must be performed by whoever first creates/collects the data set, at the time of creation/collection. It is also preferable to ensure that any unlabeled data is flagged, and the data owner alerted, so that sensitive data is not accidentally lost through lack of labeling. The labels can be assigned according to whatever internal categorization/classification system the organization uses.

- Metadata-based: The DLP can be set to restrict data to or from certain offices or personnel, specific times, locations, and so forth. These traits will be determined and associated with metadata attached to each file by the system/program when the data is created, communicated, or processed.

Implementing the DLP solution is usually a three-step process:

- Identifying sensitive data. In order to function properly, after the tool is taught which types of data it is supposed to look for, it has to be run against the currently-existing data set, in order to locate and know where those data elements are located.

- Monitoring. The DLP solution will observe the users, systems, and network for outbound traffic that contains sensitive data.

- Enforcement. When sensitive data appears to be leaving the control of the data owner, the DLP solution will respond in some fashion. This response could take any of several forms, including warning the user that the communication is against organizational policy, notifying the user's manager and/or the security office, or preventing the communication by overriding the operation, or any combination of these.

In addition to reducing the possibility of inadvertent disclosure, DLP solutions offer other benefits to the organization. These include:

- Identification of valuable assets. Because the tool must be taught to locate and know which data elements are sensitive, and initially configured against the existing data set, this process can be used in conjunction with asset inventory efforts, and even in the development of the business impact analysis (BIA), BCDR plan, and risk analysis.

- eDiscovery. As discussed in Chapter 3, ediscovery is the process of finding evidence within electronic data sets. Because the DLP tool can identify particular types of data based on definitions, labels, or metadata, it can also be employed for ediscovery purposes.

- Licensing compliance. The DLP tool might also be used to ensure that the organization doesn't violate any software licensing agreements, and act as a software license library/custodian.

The DLP solution itself will most likely include several parts, including:

- Host-based element. Each system will probably have a portion of the DLP solution, so that the solution can continue to identify and track all sensitive assets in the environment.

- Network-based element. The DLP solution will probably inspect traffic over the network to detect movement of all sensitive assets.

- Local agent. Each device used to connect to the environment will probably have some applet or instance of the DLP solution installed, in order to detect any attempted egress of the sensitive assets. This can be complicated in a BYOD environment, where the DLP will have to be platform-agnostic, in order to function

properly with all possible user devices and
systems.

DLP Complications

**DLP solutions might be stymied in an environment where all files
and traffic are encrypted; the tool might have a tough time
determining what is and what is not a sensitive asset, if it can't
read the raw data.**

Chapter 6: Academics

There are many concepts included on these exams which are simply not encountered in practice. Be prepared to see and know them. This chapter covers the topics and tries to hone in on those aspects which may show up as test questions.

OSI and TCI/IP models

The OSI seven-layer stack is a conceptual model of information technology that tries to categorize devices, protocols, and software into groups according to function. The TCP/IP Model is a similar, four-level conceptual motif; the two do not map directly and use different naming conventions with many of the same terms. The TCP/IP Model is most often seen in government use, and rarely used by the private sector. They pretty much exist only to confound and exasperate INFOSEC certification candidates.

Here's what you need to know about them:

- memorize the layer names and numbers

- memorize trace amounts of information about what takes place at each layer, focusing
on keywords from each one

- this chart can help:

Application	Application
Presentation	Transport
Session	
Transport	Internet
Network	
Data Link	Network Access
Physical	

Some mnemonics that you might find useful:

Please Do Not Teach Security People Anything

Please Do Not Try Stealing Packets, Asshole

Access Control Concepts

You will be asked questions about the different models of access control; these will come from two perspectives, the philosophical models (these will be historical conceptual designs) and the general-case implementation models. Here's what you should memorize:

Historical Designs--

- Bell-LaPadula: Designed to enforce confidentiality. A model for military/government data, where classification labels are ubiquitous; known for three basic properties, the Simple Security property, the Star property (often symbolized with an asterisk: "*"), and the Strong Star property.

- Biba: Unlike Bell-LaPadula, designed to enforce integrity, not confidentiality. Uses three properties: Simple, Star, and Invocation.

- Graham-Denning: Designed more for industry use rather than military; focuses on transactional integrity (instead of subjects/objects or confidentiality).

- Brewer-Nash: Also called the "Chinese Wall Model," designed to prevent conflicts of interest by restricting access of subjects to objects.

General-Case Implementations:

Mandatory Access Control (MAC): Based on distinct, uniform classification and labeling of objects and clearances of subjects; mostly used in government/military. Classifications are defined by the organization and enforced by the system.

Discretionary Access Control (DAC): The data owner sets permissions for objects they own, using access control lists (ACLs).

Some sources might mention "nondiscretionary access control" (as some sort of distinct model in counterpoint to DAC); do NOT bother memorizing anything about it: there is no uniform industry definition, so there won't be any questions about it on the exam.

Role-Based Access Control (RBAC): As it sounds; based on the job description/duties of the personnel within the organization.

Rule-Based Access Control (also RBAC, just to confuse you): Enforced by a central authority (usually a sysadmin); very flexible but requires a great deal of work-hours to administer. Often based on business needs and cases.

More Access Control Information

There will also be some testing material concerning current access control technology and implementations. These are some of the things you will need to know for the test:

Identity and Access Management (IAM, sometimes referred to as IdAM): The catchall phrase used to describe the discipline, solutions, and methods for provisioning, maintaining, and administering all aspects of an access control system.

IAM basics:

Identification: assigning a unique identifier to a subject (where a subject is a person or program or system that uses objects, which are usually data files or other programs). Unique identifiers usually take the form of usernames, and can assigned according to such informational elements as email address, Social Security Number, etc.

Provisioning: The first time the identifier is assigned to the subject; creating the initial user account. The identity of the subject must be confirmed in some way (such as checking a photo ID, or meeting the subject personally) before the identifier is issued.

Management: The IAM administrator must continually review subjects and identifiers to ensure that the subject still requires access, and that the subject has the proper identifier. This might be done annually or more frequently, to determine whether all account holders are still employed by the organization, or if someone's identifier needs to be changed (for instance, if the identifier is based on the last name of the subject, and the subject has changed their name because of marriage or similar trauma, the identifier might be changed to reflect the new name).

Revocation: When the subject no longer requires access, the identifier must be revoked. This can happen if the subject leaves the organization, or changes roles within the organization.

Authentication: The process of verifying that the identifier does, in fact, belong to the subject presenting it. In many cases, this is done through the use of requiring the subject to present a password when presenting the identifier.

We call the authentication elements such as passwords "factors," and they can fall into three categories:

Something you know. A password or passphrase, or some element of personal information.

Something you have. A tangible token the subject presents to the system.

Something you are. A unique biological trait of the subject, such as a fingerprint or retina pattern.

> Sensitive resources require multifactor authentication, which is the practice of requiring factors from at least two different categories of Something You Know, Something You Have, and Something You Are.

Authorization: Provisioning permitted resources to an authenticated subject. Happens after authentication, and is specific to each user, based on their access level, the permissions granted by the systems/data owner, etc.

Single Sign-On (SSO): A system in which the user can log on once and be granted access to multiple resources without repeated logons. This is usually transparent to the user, who only needs one set of credentials. SSOs can be used within an enterprise environment, or across the Internet, per the needs of the user/organization.

Kerberos: An technological SSO access-control methodology. Here's what you need to know about Kerberos-- it uses ticket-granting tickets (that's not a typo: ticket-granting tickets), and implementing it risks a single point of failure. Usually, Kerberos implementations are for internal SSOs. Don't drive yourself crazy memorizing anything else about it.

When the IAM function is outsourced to a third party, for either traditional, SSO, or federation purposes, we assign these labels to the entities involved:

- Principal. The subject, usually an individual user.

- Identity provider. The third-party IAM entity. The identity provider is in charge of provisioning, maintaining, and revoking identifiers, and performing authentication, as needed for all the principals involved, as dictated by the contracting organization(s) (usually the resource providers).

- Resource provider(s). The various entities that have systems and/or data the subjects need to access in order to perform their operational tasks.

In modern cloud computing arrangements, the identity providers often also provide additional services, such as key escrow. The popular term for these cloud identity provider is "Cloud Access Security Broker," or CASB.
A cloud service provider that also offers IAM services is not a CASB; a CASB is necessarily an independent third party.

Federation:

There are circumstances where it is advantageous for several organizations to outsource their IAM needs to a single, centralized identity provider. This is what we call "federation" (or "federated identity management," or "FedIm"), and it is usually offered in one of two forms, the web of trust and brokered identity.

In a web of trust, each party to the federation must establish a level of assurance that all the other participants are providing the same level of security, in terms of identity provision and authentication, for each of the subjects (users) involved. This includes reviewing governance from all of the other participants, and might include performing audits and other control measures. A web of trust offers a mutual trust arrangement, as each party had something to lose if any part of the web is compromised through faulty implementation; they all have a stake in the process. However, it's a cumbersome model that doesn't scale well; after a certain number of participants are in the web, any new entrant must review many policies and procedures (the governance of each of the existing members), which can be time-consuming and difficult.

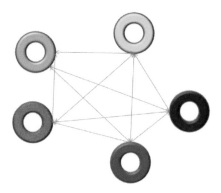

The Web of Trust Model
The donuts are all organizations taking part in the federation.
[Each one is supposed to be connected to all the rest...if there are any arrows missing, that's down to my artwork, not something to do with the model itself.]

A brokered motif is a federation model using the third party IAM provider described earlier in this section. All members of the federation agree to allow a third party to take on the IAM responsibilities for all the users of each of the member organizations. The federation members agree to establish a common set of policies and security requirements, and pay the identity broker to enforce and administer them. The brokered model is much more scalable, as any new entrant to the federation is only inspected and approved by the broker, not each of the participating entities. The brokered motif is what the aforementioned CASBs offer.

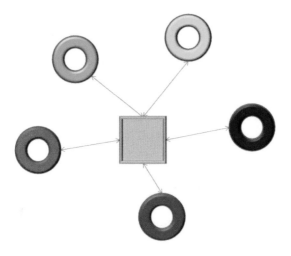

The Brokered Identity Model
Where all the donuts are the organizations participating
in the federation, and the rectangular thingy is the
contracted identity broker.

Regardless of which model is used for the
federation, the operation and function of the various
parts of the model should be transparent to the
individual users, like in SSO.

In a brokered identity federation, the identity
broker is the Identity Provider, and the various
organizations taking part in the federation are
the Resource Providers.

SAML: The Security Assertion

Most modern federations use SAML to exchange identity and authentication information. SAML (Security Assertion Markup Language) is an XML-based format and protocol for exactly this purpose. The version most often being used at the moment is SAML 2.0. In order to pass security assertions in a trusted fashion, SAML dictates the use of digital signatures and encryption; the bulk of SAML communication takes place via HTTP. SAML also requires the use of SOAP. Know this stuff for the exam.

ALE/SLE

The exams all seem to appreciate the concept of Annualized Loss Expectancy. This is a formula used as a means of stating risk in terms of a dollar value. It is completely ridiculous in the INFOSEC realm, but is a holdover from the physical security industry. It's also probably the only time you'll be called on to do math during the exam.

Here's what you need to know about it:

Single Loss Expectancy (SLE): The value of any given type of incident, occurring once, expressed in monetary terms.

Annual Rate of Occurrence (ARO): The number of times we expect a certain type of incident to occur, in one year.

Annual Loss Expectancy (ALE): The total value of loss due to that type of incident, in a year.

So ALE = ARO x SLE

This is all you need to know for the exam. What follows next is my personal view of the whole ALE/ARO/SLE concept; you can safely skip to the beginning of Chapter 7 without impacting your ability to take the test, if you don't want to read this section.

This makes sense from a physical security perspective, but really not so much from an INFOSEC perspective. Look at it this way: in the retail industry, we expect a certain amount of loss due to shoplifting. In a given store, with an average expected number of customers, we can predict a specific average percentage of loss due to theft. We know this number with some accuracy, because we have a vast trove of historical data: thefts from all retails stores, thefts from all stores in our market, thefts from stores in our local area, thefts from stores of our size and traffic level; we have this data expressed in both dollar value and quantity (number of thefts). So it's very easy to make predictions, based on current knowledge (location of store, type of merchandise, number of customers, etc.) and historical data (what has happened before, averaged and weighted). We also have another discrete fact supporting our analysis: each theft is inherently limited in value: thieves can only steal the value of the merchandise on our shelves, and only what they can carry (for this example, we're not looking at robberies, where cash from the register or safe can be taken, or pilfering by employees; we can look at those and make other ALE predictions with other data sets-- we're just viewing shoplifting as an "attack" here).

So we can determine the SLE based on the historical data and value of our merchandise. Say we expect a shoplifter to take $10 worth of merchandise, on average, in every theft.

$$SLE = \$10$$

We also know the average number of thefts per year, based on all the other data we have. Let's say, for our store in our location with our demographics, we expect 5% of our customers to shoplift per year. We also know how many customers we have per year, from various data feeds; let's say it's 100,000 people. So 5% of our customer traffic is thieves.

$$ARO = 5,000$$

Then our ALE is easy to determine: the amount of thefts multiplied by the average dollar value of each theft.

$$ALE = 5,000 \times 10 = 50,000$$

From there, it's easy to determine, from a management perspective, whether the cost of a control mechanism to prevent/deter shoplifting (a guard, or a camera, or RFID alarm tags in our merchandise, for instance) would make financial sense weighed against the expected loss. If a guard service costs us $75,000 per year, it would be stupid to choose that control, even if we were guaranteed a reduction of shoplifting to zero, because the loss itself is $25,000 less than the control.

So this makes sense in the physical realm. But in the INFOSEC regime, this doesn't work, for many reasons. First of all, we have no good historical data to use as predictors, because there is no "average" attack, no average breach, no average loss that we can expect across an industry or company. Each attack is somewhat unique. Also, each attack should not be repeatable (in all likelihood), because once we detect and respond to an attack, we should be closing the vulnerability that caused it-- in IT security, we don't leave a vulnerability exposed in perpetuity. Next, we also have no discrete limit on the value of each breach; unlike a physical theft, where the value of the loss is limited by the cost of the merchandise the thief can walk out with, an information loss can vary wildly in terms of cost to the organization...and there are many, many costs associated with a data breach that go beyond the strict value of the data lost: loss of goodwill in terms of public perception, loss due to the incident response and recovery operations, loss due to statutory fulfillment (notification and restitution, say, if the data is PII, for instance), *and* loss of the information itself. So we don't have a good grasp on SLE: we have no idea how much a given type of instance (say, "loss of data due to hacking") would cost. We also have no idea what the ARO is, because we can't predict the number of losses in a particular timeframe (we just know it won't be zero, because everyone gets breached, eventually).

Which is why, in our world, the ALE calculation is silly and pointless.

But the exams love it. So know it, and know how to calculate it.

Chapter 7: Physical Security

In our field, health and human safety is paramount. Nothing -no policy, no process, no procedure- can put health and human safety secondary to security, or even appear to do so. [Big exception? The military, and similar government programs (like protecting weapons of mass destruction). Of course.]

The reasons for this are manifold. There's the liability: any organization that places safety after security can be deemed negligent by a court/jury if any harm comes to someone in that organization's care. There's also the notion of public perception: any organization known to place safety behind security will be viewed as monstrous. Which can exacerbate the aforementioned liability aspect, too-- punitive damages can be heaped on findings of harm due to negligence, if your organization is perceived as acting in bad faith. And, of course, there is plenty of regulation that prohibits it.

So when you're designing any physical security controls, you have to keep the wetware (the meatbags-- the humans) in mind at all times, and it has to be your primary concern.

This is why we ensure all our controls that deal with emergency egress **failsafe** instead of **fail-secure.** In failsafe, people can still get out if, say, there's a fire: the emergency doors leading outside the building can always be opened, regardless if there is power in the building. If the doors were to fail-secure, instead, then all the locks would engage when power was lost, to prevent someone from taking advantage of power failure to overcome door locks. However, this does not mean all physical controls can be overcome by power outages and other similar failures: we can have fire doors that can be opened with a pushbar during exit, but do not open from the outside; this is permissible.

And this is only the case for physical security, when human safety is at stake: data does not have to be protected in the same manner, and fail-secure is perfectly allowable. Indeed, it's usually better to subject your organization to DoS if a system or utility or control fails, rather than open access to all data during fail states. In most cases, we'd rather suffer a degradation of Availability than Confidentiality.

> **You light up my life**
> INFOSEC exams just love questions about lighting. I think it has something to do with finding the few aspects of physical security that have discrete numerical values. So study up on things like the candlepower of emergency lighting, and how high above the ground is the optimal height for outdoor lighting. Seriously.

Fire. Fire, Fire, Fire

Fire is bad, because fire kills. Still, today. So we take fire very seriously. There may be multiple questions on the exam about fire and fire suppression and ways to survive a fire. Of paramount import, in every discussion about fire: health and human safety.

Fire basics: fire needs fuel, oxygen, heat, and a chemical reaction. Eliminating any of these items halts the fire. Different fire-suppression systems will target different elements of this quartet.

Know your fire extinguishers:

Class A: regular solid materials (wood, plastic, etc.)

Class B: flammable liquids (gasoline, kerosene, etc.)

Class C: electrical fires

Class D: combustible metals (magnesium, phosphorous, etc.)

Class K: kitchen fires, usually involving grease

> **What's cookin'?**
> The exams really seem to favor questions about Class K extinguishers. So definitely know that. It's a thing.

Know your pipes:

- Dry pipe: The fire suppression system does not contain water until the fire alarm or smoke detector indicates the presence of fire, at which point water is pumped into the system. Less susceptible to inadvertent releases and leaks, but takes slightly longer to deploy.

- Wet pipe: Water is present in the fire suppression system before fire is detected. The opposite risks and benefits of dry pipe.

- Sector systems: Only those sprinklers in a zone of the facility where fire is detected will activate and release water.

- Inundation systems: All sprinklers in a given area will deploy and release water throughout the area. We use inundation systems at paths of emergency egress, to protect personnel.

Know your limitations:

- We can kill fire by removing the heat, and we can remove the heat by dumping water into a room, but that also kills electronics, so we don't want to dump water into a data center, usually. We can also kill fire by removing oxygen from a room, and we can remove (actually, displace and force out) the oxygen in a room by flooding the room with an inert gas. Halon was often used for this purpose not too many decades ago, but flooding a room with halon and removing all the oxygen also kills all the people in the room (fun fact: people who breathe oxygen generally live longer than people who don't). So we don't often use halon in data center fire control systems any longer, and when we do use halon (or similar strategy) in an area where people work, there is usually (leaning toward always) "last-out" switch/button next to the door exiting the area; this is so the last person out of the room during a fire can press the button, signaling the system that it is now safe to deploy the gas. We don't build systems that put people at more risk than equipment. Ever.
Guards

Human security forces pose particular opportunities and risks. This might come up on the exam.

A guard employed by the organization will be consistent and have insight into the workings of the facility, and will recognize regular staff and employees by sight, and will be better-prepared to detect anything out of the ordinary. However, this person may also be subverted by the camaraderie and collegiality resulting from this regular interaction with the organization's personnel; the guard may be more inclined to do "favors" or overlook minor violations of policy.

My preference? Use dogs, instead.

A guard employed by an external provider might be less likely to form interpersonal connections with staff, and therefore may be more likely to have professional detachment. However, the organization will have less control over the guard, and less insight into the guard's trustworthiness.

There are, of course, hybrid methods for approaching this.

Doors and Locks

We often control physical access through the use of interior building features: doors and walls and locks and windows. The exam might include some of the following information.

Badges: Badges serve many purposes in physical security. They can hold information electronically or magnetically, and therefore be used as keys for locks. They can also be used as a detective control, because they might feature a photograph of the person who is supposed to have that badge, or they might be color-coded, with the color denoting clearance or authorization to access a specific area of the facility.

Doors: Secure doors should have a solid core, and should be rated to withstand fire. If doors are in an egress pathway, they should have pushbars or other failsafe mechanisms in the event emergency evacuation is necessary.

Mantraps: A mantrap area is an enclosed space with two doors, one on each end; each door can open only if the other is closed.

Windows: Windows should be resistant to shattering; they can be inlaid with wire mesh, or be made of some laminate (sandwiched glass and plastic). This way, if they do break for any reason, the windows will not create dangerous shards.

Video surveillance: Can be used as a detective control, but only if coverage extends throughout the facility (and often, across the property), and is being monitored in realtime, *and* there is a response capability to address threats as they are detected (guards or law enforcement). Realistically, video surveillance often better serves post-incident purposes, such as prosecution or employment action (firing someone because they did something that violated policy and was caught on camera).

Chapter 8: Incidents and Disasters

There is no standard definition of the terms "incident," "emergency," "disaster," or "event"...plenty of efforts have been made to create a uniform taxonomy, but, if you've been reading the rest of this book, you know that's a forlorn hope in our field. I could give you my definitions, but I don't want to taint the way you think about the topic, or create some imaginary hard-and-fast rule, so just try to work with whatever context each question gives you when these topics are discussed.

With that said, let's go over the things we can discuss without running afoul of definitions.

Business continuity (BC): Efforts to operate the core functions of the organization during interruptions in service. This is often done with a skeleton crew of personnel, or with reduced resources. It can happen onsite or at a relocation facility. In order to accomplish this, we need to perform a...

We are all special snowflakes
There are many ways to undertake the research necessary to write your BIA. One way that is rarely totally effective is the interview process. If you go around asking each department manager to identify the most important part of the organization, they're all going to say it's their department.

Business impact analysis (BIA): A determination of the core functions of the organization. What is it that the organization absolutely NEEDS in order to operate? What are the support functions we can do without for an extended period of time, and still remain an organization after the interruption is over? For instance, we can often jettison Human Resources functions during a period of reduced capability. In fact, we might operate better if we never had that department. Ahem.

Disaster recovery (DR): Efforts to return to normal operation after an interruption in service.

Disaster recovery plan: The documented methods and processes for conducting DR efforts. When we're talking about the documentation for BC efforts, we often refer to that as the continuity-of-operations plan (COOP).

> **In many real-world organizations, we use the terms BC and DR interchangeably, or make it one effort (BC/DR). A lot of the same personnel, offices, and resources will be involved in both types of efforts.**

Maximum allowable downtime (MAD): The amount of time (often measured in hours or days) that the organization can survive without a resource or set of resources.

Recovery Time Objective (RTO): The target time for returning to normal operations. This is measured in units of time (example: the RTO for an organization might be 96 hours). The RTO should be less than the MAD. Of course.

Recovery Point Objective (RPO): The amount of data the organization could lose in an event and still remain viable. This is measured in amount of data, either expressed in size or time (examples: the RPO for an organization might be 1 Tb, or it might be two days' worth of data).

Relocation sites: The organization should consider having an operating location some distance away from the normal facilities, where the critical business processing can take place during an extreme event. Traditionally, we want it far enough from the normal facility that it won't be affected by the same events (such as natural disasters), but not so far as to make it extremely difficult for our personnel to get there and get set up; the suggested range has usually been 250 miles. However, with cloud operations and the potential for having what amounts to a perpetual, enduring, easily-accessible backup in the cloud, traditional concepts of relocation sites are somewhat archaic and outmoded. A relocation site could be any hotel with broadband, as long as all necessary personnel have devices that can handle critical workloads (organization-issued laptops with sufficient access controls and other protections should probably suffice).

Still, for the exam, these are the types of relocation sites you should know:

Hot site: A facility fully equipped with all components necessary to resume critical functions upon arrival. All hardware is of like type and capability as the normal production environment, and all software is installed, updated, and patched, and all data is populated (or easily uploaded quickly). Utilities are set up and available at the flick of a switch. Preferably, it's just a mirror of your production facility. And maybe some snacks.

Warm site: The hardware may be available, and utilities are set up, but you may have to install software and data.

Cold site: A bare-bones facility; just a space with connection ports. You'll need to bring/buy all necessary hardware and software.

Obviously, price dictates which type of site an organization will use, with hot sites being the most expensive.

Some exams might include a question about mobile relocation sites; basically, this is just an RV equipped with machines. It's a silly, expensive, and awkward method for a relocation site. The question will probably ask about fuel or something similarly obtuse.

Backups (incremental/differential/full) and vs. the cloud: In legacy environments, especially those where digital archives did not exist, we had various methods of creating backups, because backing everything up in continual fashion was not a viable option; backup technologies were too slow and expensive. So the exam might include questions about backup methods. These include:

> Full backup: Just like it sounds. A total reproduction of all the data in the production environment (even with the word "full," it usually indicates only the data, not all the executable software).

> Incremental backup: Only the data since the last incremental backup is copied. Example: if we do full backups on Saturday night, and we do an incremental backup on Monday night, we back up everything from Sunday and Monday, and then if we do another incremental backup Wednesday night, we only include everything from Tuesday and Wednesday. It's the smallest amount of backup data of the different methods.

> Differential backup: Only the data since the last full backup is copied. Example: if we do full backups on Saturday night, and we do a differential backup on Monday night, we include everything from Sunday and Monday, and then if we do another differential backup on Wednesday night, we include everything from Sunday, Monday, Tuesday, and Wednesday.

Incident response

This could be the topic of an entire book. Well, okay-- there are entire books written on just this topic. You might want to read one or two of them. But I'll try to include just the things you'll need to know for the test in this section.

Triage of incident

Our immediate actions in response to given event are going to depend almost entirely on the circumstances, with some slight input from our local policy and overall context. Before we act, we need to know what we're dealing, so we have to determine what the actual event is, what the risk associated with it are, and the potential benefits and losses that could result from each of our policy actions in response. This can't be a hasty decision, because a wrong response could be even more damaging than the event itself. The security team should evaluate the event, the security manager should come up with a set of possible responses, and senior management should make the decision on which course of action to take.

IR team

It's important to have the right set of skills and capabilities on the incident response team. Be sure to involve representatives from management, the IT department (preferably personnel from both the sysadmin and network administration sides of the house), the security office, the legal department, Human Resources, Public Relations, and, if possible, someone from the administrative team (it's crucial to have proper documentation and a good record of the event and response for reporting and after-action activities). The composition of the team should be flexible to meet the challenges of any given event.

Check out this awesome article about the initial steps of incident response. It's pretty old, but I hear the author is an extremely handsome man:

http://www.symantec.com/connect/articles/moments-notice-immediate-steps-incident-handling

Incident kit (should also serve as your BC/DR kit)

Make sure you have a portable container (preferably watertight, fireproof, and weather-resistant) which contains a few important things:

- configuration management documentation, including current baseline with all patches and updates (plus the software to match)

- contact rosters for key personnel

- copies of the COOP/DR plan

- batteries

- flashlight

- water

- writing instruments and pads of paper

- a camera

- possibly, backup short-distance communication (walkie-talkies)

All documentation should be in both hardcopy and electronic forms.

LE involvement

Senior management should make the decision (or at the very least, be informed) when law enforcement should be asked to address the incident. In some cases, this "decision" will be pro forma, because statutory and regulatory requirements mandate notification (for instance, if your organization ever discovers child pornography on any resources owned by the organization, involving law enforcement is not an option, it is a requirement).

Generators

The major concerns with generators will be fuel and exhaust. Fuel needs to be stored away from locations where it may be affected by motor vehicle accidents, and needs to be refreshed about every six months. Fumes need to be vented properly so as not to affect personnel, especially if the generator is located in a contained area (such as a basement or parking garage, or basement parking garage).

Honeypots

The legality and efficacy of honeypots (dummy target systems, usually set in the DMZ as a means to attract and distract attackers, while gathering information about attacks) varies widely, depending on jurisdiction. In the US, honeypots can actually attenuate your organization's ability to prosecute attackers, because, depending on how they are deployed and configured, they might constitute an invitation to enter your network (much like the "attractive nuisance" concept a swimming pool in your backyard poses). In some other jurisdictions, they are a wonderful way to hammer attackers with impunity. See also....

Hackback

The notion of "he hit me first!" does not quite exist in the IT realm; we can't attack our attackers via the Internet. At least not in the US.

Investigations

In order to determine the best response option, the optimal way of fixing the root cause of the problem, and collection of potential evidence, an investigation is often conducted. Investigations are undertaken in order to answer those elemental questions surrounding the incident: Who, What, Why, How, and When.

Forensics

All data collected during investigatory activity should be considered potential evidence; long-term response actions might include criminal prosecution or civil lawsuit (or both), so how the evidence is collected is extremely important. Many aspects of forensic investigation are best left to professional with specific training in those aspects of the field, including formal interviewing techniques and electronic data collection. Certifications and licensing are available for these, as well. An internal IR team without people trained in these specialties is often better served by contracting out these services to companies and individuals who have these skillsets and perform these activities on a regular basis.

Evidence

All data collected during an investigation can be considered evidence, and may be used later in court. Therefore, it's very important to preserve and protect this data in as close to its original state as possible. However, there is a prevailing myth in our field that has confused this issue somewhat: it was long held (and advised, by professionals) that original electronic sources and data sets were never to be manipulated, because that would render the evidence inadmissible in court. This is simply not true: evidence can be modified for analysis (think: blood samples destroyed while testing for DNA; the results are still admissible, even though the original evidence doesn't even exist anymore), as long as all steps and methods are rigorously and comprehensively documented in extreme detail.

Evidence may have to be presented to the court, so evidence should have these characteristics:

- Authentic: What is presented is actual evidence collected from the scene, or results of analysis of evidence derived from the scene.

- Understandable: The court will likely not understand the evidence with the level of expertise that an INFOSEC practitioner can comprehend, so it's your duty to be able to explain it in a way a layperson would be comfortable with.

- Supporting: Your evidence should tell your narrative. This does not mean you should withhold evidence that counters your explanation of the incident, only that you are able to explain the situation and circumstances thoroughly.

- Complete: Again, you cannot keep information from the court, nor should you want to. Trying to isolate pieces of evidence in a selective manner makes your story less coherent and believable; tell the whole story, using all the evidence.

Chain of custody

As evidence is collected, it must be safeguarded and accounted for at all times. We call this practice maintaining the chain of custody: a person is assigned to monitor and control the evidence from the time it is collected until it is presented to the court.

The chain of custody should be accurately documented, and should include:

- The identities of anyone who had access to the evidence from the time of collection until presentation.

- Where, when, and how the evidence was collected.

- Where and how the evidence was stored and controlled.

- How the evidence was analyzed, and by whom.

Chapter 9: Taking Tests

Multiple-choice tests gauge exactly one facet of you as a person: your ability to take multiple-choice tests. Some people can know all the material on the test, to the point where they could lecture for an hour on the topic mentioned in any single question...but still do poorly on the test. Some people can get a passing grade on an exam without even knowing the subject, just because they are extremely good at taking multiple-choice tests.

Where do the smart people fail? How do the mediocre people pass?

Points of failure:

- RTFQ. Read. The. Fucking. Question. Also known as, and even more useful: Read The FULL Question. Many times, the question can include clues to the answer, just in the wording of the question itself, or in the various answers. Also: READ THE FULL ANSWER. I can't stress this enough: many of the answers on these multiple-choice tests include several correct options, but only one answer is the "most correct." Read ALL the possible selections before choosing the one you think is the best. Sometimes, in haste to finish the test, you may be tempted to choose the first answer, because it's right. That is the WRONG thing to do.

DON'T PANIC: If you run across a nonsensical question on an ISC2 test, it may be a question ISC2 is experimenting with, to determine its suitability for future tests. ISC2 exams all contain a few of these practice questions, which are not included in your test score (regardless of whether you get them "right").

- Overthinking the question. Each question on every exam is the result of long, intense workshopping by professionals. Which means that every question is about as banal and straightforward as it could be made. Sometimes, it will seem so straightforward that you'll think it's a trick question. It usually isn't. Read what's there, and answer THAT question...not the question you think it might be. Again: RTFQ.

- Misreading the question. The exception to the aforementioned Overthinking advice is the "Not" question: the question that contains a straightforward query with three correct and very straightforward answers...and one other, bizarre answer that is actually the right one, because the question included the word "not." Like:

"When placing a device in the DMZ, which of these do you want to be sure not to do?
A) remove all default accounts
B) close unnecessary ports
C) run strong authentication
D) retain all libraries and services"

The answer is, of course, D....but if you misread the question, all the other answers seem correct, because those are what you *should* do when configuring machines for the DMZ, while D is what you should *not* do. So, again: RTFQ. I am not sure how to emphasize this enough, but I'll try:

RTFQ

- Changing your answer. Scientific reviews of testtaking habits and trends have demonstrated, time and again, that people taking tests are most likely to change a correct answer to an incorrect one, instead of vice-versa. Trust your gut, for the most part. If you really, really think you made a mistake on first pass, or something reminds you of the right answer, then change your original selection. But know that this inclination is usually wrong.

How to pass:

- Know what material is being tested. This is different than knowing the material: this is knowing what material to know. See: What Material To Know, later in this chapter.

- Go in with the right amount of anxiety. Passing or failing this exam has consequences, so you are right to take it seriously, which means a good amount of trepidation. But if you go in frightened, you can panic and freak yourself out, and fail because you're not thinking clearly. If, however, you don't take it seriously, or think it's going to be easy, and go into the

> We're a field of experts...which means we disagree on just about everything; ask five INFOSEC practitioners about certain topics, and you'll get six opinions. Consensus is rare...so tests avoid questions with known gray areas. This can help you study for the exam, because you can be fairly certain that it won't include questions where there is widespread disagreement.

exam with a false sense of confidence, you can miss

how questions are worded, or which of the answers is "most" correct. So: go in with some tension, some respect for how difficult the test process will be, but not to the point where you're going to cease thinking clearly.

- Practice tests. If possible, look up as many test banks and sample tests as you can, and practice taking. Be aware that many samples do NOT match the actual test created by the certifying bodies, and are therefore not a perfect demonstration of how you'll perform. But more testing will make you more confident, and may expose some problem areas you need to study more.

- Be aware of previous answers. The answers to many questions on the exam are contained in other questions; even something as simple as an acronym you momentarily forgot might be spelled out in another question. Be prepared to scroll back through the test to adjust your answer if you find the solution in a future question. This should be one of the rare exceptions to the aforementioned Don't Change Your Answer advice.

- Pare down the list. Almost all of these exam questions are multiple-choice...which means the question-writers had to craft something that is accurate, well-known, and can have four responses. Often, this is quite impossible-- so they sacrifice the last aspect. Therefore, many questions have one wild response that cannot possible be correct, and then one that is probably wrong, and two that are possibly correct. That leaves you with a reasonable 50/50 chance of success, even if you can't figure out what The Right Answer is. Eliminate badness to reveal goodness.

- Don't use order bias. The first answer is not more correct than the others, but it's the first you read, and if all four answers sound like they could satisfy the question, you might be more likely to give credence to the one at the top of the list...or, worse, you might fail to heed the RTFQ advice, and select the first answer because it seems right, without looking at the others. So one of my students gave me an excellent piece of advice for multiple-choice tests: read the answers from D to A, bottom to top, instead of the normal order. Love this. It's genius.

What Material to Know:

ISC2 (CISSP-ISSAP/ISSEP/ISSMP, CCSP, CAP, CSSLP, CCFP, HCISSP): if you're taking an ISC2 exam, all the material on the exam will be included or mentioned in the ISC2 Student Guide for that particular certification. ISC2 certifications are broken down into Domains with specific content areas. As of 2016, ISC2 has begun publishing the weights of each domain, as reflected by number of questions on the exam. While not yet available on the ISC2 website, these have been made public to ISC2 members and candidates, so I will include them here:

CAP Domains	Weight
1. Risk Management Framework (RMF)	20%
2. Categorization of Information Systems	8%
3. Selection of Security Controls	13%
4. Security Control Implementation	10%
5. Security Control Assessment	19%
6. Information System Authorization	13%
7. Monitoring of Security Controls	17%
Total	100%

CISSP Domains	Weight
1. Security and Risk Management	16%
2. Asset Security	10%
3. Security Engineering	12%
4. Communication and Network Security	12%
5. Identity and Access Management	13%
6. Security Assessment and Testing	11%
7. Security Operations	16%
8. Software Development Security	10%
Total	100%

CISSP ISSMP Domains	Weight
1. Security Leadership and Management	38%
2. Security Lifecycle Management	21%
3. Security Compliance Management	14%
4. Contingency Management	12%
5. Law, Ethics and Incident Management	15%
Total	100%

SSCP Domains	Weight
1. Access Control	16%
2. Security Operations and Administration	17%
3. Risk Identification, Monitoring and Analysis	12%
4. Incidence Response, and Recovery	13%
5. Cryptography	9%
6. Network and Communication Security	16%
7. Systems and Applications Security	17%
Total	**100%**

CCSP Domains	Weight
1. Architectural Concepts & Design Requirements	19%
2. Cloud Data Security	20%
3. Cloud Platform & Infrastructure Security	19%
4. Cloud Application Security	15%
5. Operations	15%
6. Legal & Compliance	12%
Total	**100%**

CISSP-ISSEP Domains	Weight
1. Systems Engineering Processes and Technical Management	16%
2. The Systems Security Engineering Process	48%
3. Systems Security Engineering in Risk Management	16%
4. Applied Security Practices	20%
Total	**100%**

HCISSP Domains	Weight
1. Healthcare Industry	10%
2. Regulatory Environment	16%
3. Privacy and Security in Healthcare	26%
4. Information Governance and Risk Management	17%
5. Information Risk Assessment	16%
6. Third-Party Risk Management	15%
Total	**100%**

CCFP Domains	Weight
1. Legal and Ethical Principles	12%
2. Investigations	20%
3. Forensic Science	20%
4. Digital Forensics	28%
5. Application Forensics	12%
6. Hybrid and Emerging Technologies	8%
Total	**100%**

CISSP-ISSAP Domains	Weight
1. Identity and Access Management Architecture	19%
2. Security Operations Architecture	17%
3. Infrastructure Security	19%
4. Architect for Governance, Compliance, and Risk Management	16%
5. Security Architecture Modeling	14%
6. Architect for Application Security	15%
Total	**100%**

CSSLP Domains	Weight
1. Secure Software Concepts	13%
2. Secure Software Requirements	14%
3. Secure Software Design	16%
4. Secure Software Implementation/Programming	16%
5. Secure Software Testing	14%
6. Secure Lifecycle Management	10%
7. Software Deployment, Operations, Maintenance	9%
8. Supply Chain and Software Acquisition	8%
Total	100%

ISACA (CISM, CISA): ISACA exams are diagrammed by number of questions on the test, related to specific content areas. So, for instance, on the CISM exam, as of the time of this writing, the breakdown of questions is:

Domain 1—Information Security Governance (24%)
Domain 2—Information Risk Management and Compliance (33%)
Domain 3—Information Security Program Development and Management (25%)
Domain 4—Information Security Incident Management (18%)

[From the ISACA website: http://www.isaca.org/certification/cism-certified-information-security-manager/job-practice-areas/pages/default.aspx]

When studying for an ISACA test, you can game out the number of questions you can expect on the exam, versus which material you're more comfortable with, and what you need to brush up on. Using the CISM example, if you're very knowledgeable in the Incident Management realm, but weak on Risk Management, it would behoove you to spend much more time studying the latter, as the test is weighted more in that discipline.

CompTIA (Network+, Security+):

Like the other certifying bodies, CompTIA provides a breakdown, by domain, of each of their tests. You can access the exam objectives and samples via the CompTIA website (https://certification.comptia.org/certifications/security and https://certification.comptia.org/certifications/network).

As of the time of this writing, the Network+ test breakdown is:

Network Architecture 22%
Network Operations 20%
Network Security 18%
Troubleshooting 24%
Industrial Standards, Practices and Network Theory 16%

The Security+ exam objectives are:

Network Security 20%
Compliance and Operational Security 18%
Threats and Vulnerabilities 20%
Application, Data and Host Security 15%
Access Control and Identity Management 15%
Cryptography 12%

The Exam Objectives documents for both tests are extremely thorough and detailed, allowing you to find the area(s) where you might need to study more before taking the exam. I particularly recommend reviewing the Acronym List (more like a list of terms) for each test to help you determine what you already know and what you might need to brush up on. You have to register to get the information, but it's free.

> **Knowing what to know: a bias.**
> The exams lean heavily toward practice and regulation from the United States; most of the certifications were created there. A big exception: there will be quite a few questions about the EU Data Protection Directive. But that's the exception.

Repeating History:

In many cases, the material on the exam was crafted and set a long time before you're actually going to take the test, so it will include concepts, technology, and even statutes that have been superseded or made obsolete already. This is why you have to know what is being *tested*, not what the real-world perspective is, for many topics. For instance, in the ISC2 tests, as of the time of this writing, the EU Data Directive (Directive 94/46/EC) comprises a significant portion of the testable material, even though it was replaced in May of 2016. So while you should be familiar with the current law (the EU General Data Protection Regulation) for your professional duties, you'll have to know the old law for the exam. This is not my fault. Really.

Likewise, events that could not have been predicted when the test was written have changed the legal and technical landscapes of our world in dramatic fashion. The Heartbleed vulnerability and the Brexit vote are a couple of examples of this. So you might see questions about SSL and how to treat British members of the EU on the exam, which might be confusing. Remember, context is important, so stay aware of these things and try to be familiar with recent history.

Comprehension Exhaustion

Some of the exams are overwhelming; they cover so much material from so many different disciplines, that no one person could be expected to know all the subject matter thoroughly and completely with a degree of expertise, even if they spent a lifetime in the field of INFOSEC. This is particularly true of the CISSP, but all the tests have this trait, to greater or lesser extent. For instance, it's unlikely that a networking engineer will have a deep understanding of the material dealing with policy, or that a system administrator would know all the ins and outs of physical security.

Therefore, it's not in your best interest to try to understand every topic on the test; a deep comprehension of all the elements is just unlikely and unwieldy; you could drive yourself crazy trying to learn all the things that you know you don't know. Instead, it's much better to learn the essential elements of the material, just enough to pass the exam. Use this technique when dealing with the questions, as well.

For instance, let's pick the topic of SAML. If you already have a total understanding of SAML, pretend you don't. Instead of learning all the details of SAML, how it works, its history, and how to put it into practice, instead recall the specific traits of SAML discussed in this book.

We know that SAML:

- Has to do with identification and authentication of identity assertions.

- Is used in federation models.

- Is based on XML.

Using just these characteristics, we can deal with questions related to the topic of SAML in a straightforward way. Let's say you get to a question with SAML in it. To start with, we don't even need to know what the question is:

"Xxxxxx xxxxxx xxxxxxxx xxx xxxx xxxxx xxxx SAML."

Already, we should be thinking, "identification/authentication," "federation," and "XML."

Then READ THE FULL QUESTION:

"Which of these purposes could be addressed through the use of SAML?"

This is wonderful: we're already expecting three different possible terms that could be used in a correct answer, so we're prepared to focus on answers that include those terms. So we review all the answers:

"A. Creating encrypted tunnels for remote users."

"B. Sanitization of sensitive material online."

"C. Designing attack-resistant APIs."

"D. Creating a web of trust for multiple organizations."

Unfortunately, in this example, none of the answers include the specific terms we were expecting. However, each of the answers should trigger our memory of other terms related to each of those topics. If we go through each one, we see:

"A. Encrypted tunnels....that should be SSL/TLS, L2TP, or PPTP."

"B. Sanitization...that should include physical destruction, degaussing, overwriting, or cryptoshredding."

"C. Strong APIs....that could involve the OWASP Top 10, or software testing methods..."

"D. Web of trust...that's a federation model."

Boom-- Answer D is the one that's got the specific term we were expecting when we first saw SAML, so that's the one to go with.

Additional Resources

This book shouldn't serve as your standalone preparation for the exam; you should find more detailed sources for those topics you don't quite feel comfortable with.

These are some good resources that either I've used to study for the various tests, or that my students and colleagues have suggested.

Charles Cresson Wood: "Information Security Policies Made Easy"

Wood has been publishing this title for over a decade, and recent editions sell for exorbitant amounts. However, you should be able to find older editions, a few versions back, that are affordable, and, realistically, the concepts related to INFOSEC policy creation haven't changed all that much, so you won't be missing anything.

Bruce Schneier: Anything

Absolutely anything you read by Schneier will be informative and entertaining; he's an outstanding genius, and a great writer. He also challenges a lot of assumptions in the INFOSEC world. Perhaps best known for his creation of the Blowfish algorithm and his work on Twofish, there isn't any aspect of security he's not well-versed in.

These books, in particular, are some of his better sellers:

"Secrets and Lies: Digital Security in a Networked World"

"Schneier on Security"

You can also subscribe to his blog online, or have his frequent listserv emailed to you: https://www.schneier.com/crypto-gram

The SANS Reading Room:
https://www.sans.org/reading-room/
 Every candidate for a SANS exam has the opportunity to earn additional distinction for their certification by publishing a paper in the Reading Room. There are essays on almost every possible topic, and while some of them are better than others, they are all free to read. Worth taking a look at, if there's something you're not clear on.

Verizon Data Breach Reports:
http://www.verizonenterprise.com/DBIR/
 Verizon has been assembling their Data Breach Reports for several years, and they are insightful and interesting. They are mainly based on self-reported data, so their conclusions about frequency of types of attacks might be somewhat distorted, but the information they contain is worthwhile nonetheless.

Shon Harris: "CISSP Practice Exams"
 Shon Harris built an empire out of teaching candidates how to pass the CISSP exam. While she died before the conversion of the CISSP CBK from 10 domains to 8, the material isn't all that much more different in the current version, so any of her work that you can get your hands on should still be quite informative and useful.

Sybex Study Guide: "CISSP: Certified Information Systems Security Professional Study Guide"
 I've heard mixed reviews from students who have used this book to study for the CISSP exam.

However, it's quite affordable, and seems to have a lot of good information.

Syngress Study Guide: "CISSP Study Guide, Second Edition"
Again, students have had many opinions about the efficacy of this book, but it doesn't seem too pricey.

Sybex Study Guide: "CCSP (ISC)2 Certified Cloud Security Professional Official Study Guide"
I wrote this one, so I'm kinda biased. I think it's pretty good, though. It comes out in April, 2017. https://www.amazon.com/Certified-Cloud-Security-Professional-Official/dp/1119277418

NIST SP 800 series
All of these documents are online, for free. If there is any particular topic you're hesitant about, feel free to check them out.

McGraw Hill CISSP Exam Prep quizzes online: https://www.mhprofessionalresources.com//sites/CISSPExams/index.php
McGraw Hill offers some free online courseware, including audio files and review questions, as long as you register.

CCCure sample questions: https://www.cccure.org/
Requires registration, but many students praise it

Wiley CISSP practice tests:
http://www.wiley.com/WileyCDA/WileyTitle/produ
ctCd-1119252288.html
Not free, but I've heard the questions are comprehensive and very similar to what actually appears on the exam.

"Down the Security Rabbithole":
http://podcast.wh1t3rabbit.net/
An absolutely outstanding free podcast. Covers current events in the INFOSEC field, often features interesting guests, and is always entertaining.

ISC2 webcasts.
If you're a member of ISC2 already (if you have one of the many certifications they offer, you're a member), you can check out their webinars, which are usually 1-3 hours long, with one speaker per hour, and each webinar is oriented on a specific topic. They're informative and free, and the whole archive is available online.

BitGlass webinars: http://www.bitglass.com/events-
webinars
BitGlass is a CASB, and they offer intriguing webinars on a variety of topics on a regular basis.

Good luck.
Relax.
Do great

Made in the USA
Middletown, DE
02 July 2019